Myth and the Crisis
of Historical Consciousness

MYTH AND THE CRISIS
OF HISTORICAL CONSCIOUSNESS

Edited by

Lee W. Gibbs
and
W. Taylor Stevenson

Published by

SCHOLARS PRESS

for

The American Academy of Religion

Distributed by
SCHOLARS PRESS
University of Montana
Missoula, Montana 59801

MYTH AND THE CRISIS
OF HISTORICAL CONSCIOUSNESS

Edited by

Lee W. Gibbs
and
W. Taylor Stevenson

Library of Congress Cataloging and Publication Data:

Myth and the crisis of historical consciousness.

Essays from the seminar held during the annual meet-
ings of the American Academy of Religion, 1972-1974.
Includes bibliographical references and index.
1. Myth — Addresses, essays, lectures. 2. History —
Philosophy — Addresses, essays, lectures. I. Gibbs,
Lee W. II. Stevenson, W. Taylor. III. American
Academy of Religion.
BL304.M86   901   75-33049
ISBN 0-89130-053-8

Printed in the United States of America
1 2 3 4 5
Printing Department
University of Montana
Missoula, Montana 59801

TABLE OF CONTENTS

Contributors

CORNELIA DIMMITT CHURCH is Assistant Professor, Theology Department, Georgetown University, Washington, D.C. She is currently editing and translating a volume of selected myths from Sanskrit epics and *purāṇas*.

LEE W. GIBBS is Associate Professor, Department of Religious Studies, The Cleveland State University, Cleveland, Ohio. He is currently at work on a book, tentatively entitled *The Mystery of Evil*.

ADELE B. MCCOLLUM is Assistant Professor, Department of Philosophy and Religion, Montclair State College, Upper Montclair, New Jersey. She formerly practiced psychiatric nursing in public and private institutions. Her continuing research interest is in the area of developing a Jungian methodology of history.

RICHARD A. RAY is Editor of the John Knox Press, Atlanta, Georgia. He is currently at work on making a critical evaluation of the work of Rudolf Bultmann, and his followers and critics.

W. TAYLOR STEVENSON is Professor of Philosophical Theology, Seabury-Western Theological Seminary, Evanston, Illinois. He is the editor of the *Anglican Theological Review*, and his continuing research interest is in the field of the relationship of history and myth.

GEORGE WECKMAN is Associate Professor, Philosophy Department, Ohio University, Athens, Ohio. He made a study-tour of India during the Winter of 1974-1975 in order to examine Indian iconography.

JAMES B. WIGGINS is Professor of Religion, Department of Religion, Syracuse University, Syracuse, New York. He is editor of and contributor to *Religion and Story: Explorations and Reflections* (Harper and Row, Forum Books, 1975).

Introduction

I

THE essays published in this volume have emerged out of the Myth Seminar sponsored by the American Academy of Religion during the years 1972-74. All the papers focus upon the general theme of the seminar, namely, "myth and the crisis of historical consciousness." The sustained exploration of this theme proved to be a most fruitful area of inquiry, for it opened a path leading directly to the nature and origins of what seems to us to be the present moral, intellectual, and spiritual crisis of civilization in the West.

"Historical consciousness" in the narrow sense refers to the self-conscious attitude and methodology of the "scientific historian." The phrase can also be taken in the more general sense of understanding man and reality in historical categories. In our judgment there is, using either or both senses of the term, a crisis of historical consciousness in the West.

A fundamental presupposition of this seminar, then, is that there is a contemporary crisis in historical consciousness. Is this indeed the case? The affirmative answer to that question is developed explicitly and implicitly in the essays which follow. However, it might be useful at this point to indicate briefly what it is that leads us to make this presupposition.

Possibly the most powerful challenge to historical consciousness has been the work of Sigmund Freud and Carl Jung, and their respective followers. They have challenged in an irrefutable way the ideas so essential to post-Enlightenment historical consciousness: history is linear and oriented to the future; it proceeds upon the basis of rational cause and effect; it is the privileged form of human understanding; etc. Whatever our judgment about the usefulness of Freud or Jung, they have shown us what we should not have forgotten, namely, that an exclusively linear, empirical, rationalized appreciation of experience is simplistic. That simplistic approach has marked much of the methodology and practice of scientific history, and hence the challenges of Freud and Jung contribute to a crisis in historical consciousness.

A second major challenge to historical consciousness is the general social and cultural experience in the West since World War I. It has been a catena of brutalizing wars, genocides, and betrayals by men and movements. The result of this general experience is reflected in the active distaste for the study of history found in so many Americans. It is reflected artistically in the influential work of the dramatist Samuel Beckett who speaks of "accursed time," and meaning by that exactly the ongoing, event-filled, causally-related course of human experience which is the métier of the historian. It is impossible to quantify this diffused social and cultural disenchantment with history, but it is safe to say it makes a significant contribution to the contemporary crisis in historical consciousness.

A third major component in the contemporary crisis in historical consciousness is, ironically, the discipline of the history of religions. The history of religions has made available to us the experience of other religions and cultures in such a way that we can appreciate them in a positive way. Most of these religions and cultures do not depend upon historical consciousness for their ordering of experience; or, at the very least, they do not do so in the modern Western way. This development has the effect of relativizing historical consciousness, and thereby challenges its typical claim to be a priviledged form of understanding. This challenge, both in its academic and popularized forms, is another significant dimension in the contemporary crisis in historical consciousness.

These three factors — psychoanalysis, twentieth century social and cultural experience, and the history of religions — have brought about the crisis in historical consciousness. All of these factors will be explored, expanded, and related in the essays which follow. The prognosis which will emerge in the essays is not necessarily that we are experiencing the demise of historical consciousness, but that the way in which we have come to *conceptualize* that consciousness is seriously inadequate. And, as always, inadequate conceptualization leads to inadequate practice.

II

The questions and problems mentioned above are explored and discussed by the authors of the essays in this book. The papers by W. Taylor Stevenson and Lee W. Gibbs have been placed first, for they deal in the greatest detail with the meaning and background of what is meant by the crisis of historical consciousness and how it relates to the decline and revival of interest in myth. The papers by Stevenson, Gibbs, Cornelia D. Church, and to some extent that by Richard A. Ray, are concerned with a renewal and reinterpretation of traditional Jewish and Christian myths and symbols.

The papers by Church and Ray presuppose the work of the depth psychologist Carl G. Jung with respect to the relationship between myth, history, and the archetypes of the collective unconscious. However, it is in the essays by James Wiggins and Adele B. McCollum that the Jungian contribution to the problems under discussion are most carefully and fully set forth in terms of "psychohistory" and "mythohistory."

The paper by George Weckman has been placed last because, in the context of his brief survey of the varieties of interpretation, analysis, and reduction of myth, the author sets forth a strong critique of psychological interpretations of myth in general and of the Jungian interpretation of myth in particular. In addition, two of Weckman's closing observations constitute a fitting, open-ended conclusion for this volume of essays addressed to the theme of myth and the crisis of historical consciousness. First, Weckman argues that there are many reasons why myths should lose significance or change in their modes of influence or apprehension, only one of which is the rising or shifting of attention to history. Second, Weckman argues that, granted the partial collapse of modern historical consciousness, the revival or rejuvenation of mythic consciousness is only one among several alternatives.

III

The seminar for which the papers in this volume were prepared was originally conceived along the lines of a small task force attacking a problem area of common interest. The seminar brought together scholars who approach the study and interpretation of myth from different disciplinary perspectives and fields of specialization. In spite of the interdisciplinary flavor of the seminar, all participants — including the contributors to this book — were united in two respects. First, they were presently involved in some kind of research, writing, and teaching on the topic of myth. And second, they were all seeking in their own way for some kind of constructive reinterpretation or reappropriation of myth in categories which might prove meaningful to contemporary men and women in the West.

The papers were written and distributed to the members of the seminar several months before they were scheduled for presentation at the Annual Meeting of the American Academy of Religion. After careful study by all of the seminar participants, written critiques were then submitted to the authors of individual papers. At this point the essays were rewritten in the light of these critiques and then redistributed at least one month before the official convocation of the seminar. As a final preparatory step, the papers were read and criticized a second time by participants in the seminar before the seminar was actually convened.

At the regularly scheduled sessions of the seminar, each author distributed a one-page abstract on his or her paper and then made a ten-minute presentation on the general methodology and content of the paper, the nature of the criticisms of the first draft, and the modifications made in the subsequent draft as a result of reflection upon those criticisms. These ten-minute presentations were followed by longer discussions between the authors of individual papers and all members of the seminar. Finally, the discussion was opened up to include the general audience which was present at each session.

Before the papers in this volume were collected for publication, they were all, to one degree or another, revised a second time in the light of the questions, comments, and discussion generated at the official convocations of the seminar.

The editors wish to express their appreciation to all those members of the seminar who cooperated in meeting the rigorous requirements and deadlines demanded by the project. The editors also wish to thank those individuals who so willingly criticized the papers of others while electing not to write papers of their own.

LEE W. GIBBS
W. TAYLOR STEVENSON

Myth and the Crisis of Historical Consciousness

W. Taylor Stevenson

ASSUMING the general orientation outlined in the first part of the Introduction to this volume, this essay discusses the following questions. First, how shall we understand history and historical consciousness? Second, what are the understandings of myth which have emerged during the past generation, and what is the role of myth in the construction of human meaning? Third, how might we understand the relationship between history and myth in order to respond creatively to our contemporary cultural and social disruption?

The position which emerges in the following pages is, partly explicitly and partly implicitly, a critical-conservative one; critical in that it recognizes the need for dialectic and reconstruction, and conservative in that it takes the central traditions of the West, and of the Christian faith, with great seriousness. It is clearly recognized that, no more than alternative positions, the correctness of the position advanced here cannot be established by logic alone. Rather, this position is assumed, first, because I *find* myself within this tradition; it is at hand. Following Paul Ricoeur, I believe it is necessary to begin from what is near, rather than from what is at a distance. Second, I assume this position because I have made a wager that a critical-conservative handling, a reappropriation, of Western and Christian traditions will pay off in greater fruitfulness than will other traditions, and including a greater fruitfulness in the creative appropriation of certain aspects at least of those other traditions.

Further, I would like to enter an even more personal note. This has to do with the issue as to whether, without entering into some kind of intellectual and personal disjunction, one can be a historian and Christian believer. I believe Harvey is correct in his *The Historian and the Believer* in focusing upon this as a central issue, although I am not completely satisfied with the way in which he handles the issue.[1] An overarching concern of this paper, and my work as a whole, is to deal with that issue.

The situation is complex, to say the least. Another way to express and extend this is to draw upon Ricoeur and say that for me too my overarching concern is the "expectancy of a new Word, of a new tidings of the Word"[2] in response to which it will be possible to "leave off all demands and listen."[3]

I. How Shall We Understand History?

I understand history as a peculiar way of apprehending and ordering the totality of human experience, past, present, and (by anticipation) future. It is marked by a number of highly significant and distinctive characteristics; for example, its primary orientation is to the future rather than the past, it places a very high valuation upon the new and the unique, it exalts man by insisting upon his freedom and responsibility, it (consequently) "explains" evil primarily in terms of the Adamic myth, it places a high evaluation upon the created empirical order, etc. These and other characteristics are, if you will, points upon the hermeneutical circle of history. History has been and is the dominant (not exclusive) mode of perceiving experience, searching for the "real," and structuring the self in the West. As far as I can tell, it is in the contemporary world one of the three fundamental ways of perceiving experience, the other two being the archaic and that represented by the various Eastern spiritualities. History is not *absolutely* unique to the West. For example, archaic man recognizes what *we* call history to this extent: "it" (our Western "history") is a form without content. There are *analogies* between at least some points on the hermeneutical circle of history and other articulations of experience. Nevertheless, history (all of the points on the circle, taken as an interdependent whole) is a highly distinctive way of perceiving personal and social experience peculiar to the Western tradition. Even more dubious than declaring everyone to be "anonymous Christians" is the declaration that really everyone understands experience the way we do in the West. We do them the "honor" of making them "anonymous historians"!

The term "history" is used in several interdependent and overlapping ways. The context of the use of the term usually indicates which sense is intended. *Sometimes* the use of the term history can be taken in more than one of its senses, and it does make a great deal of difference because of the close interdependence of the various uses of the term.

History can be understood as "historical consciousness." This is the way in which the term has been used in the first paragraphs of this section. This is a consciousness which can be distinguished from other forms of consciousness, e.g., the archaic. It is a consciousness which has the characteristics which we mentioned above, a particular way of perceiving the "out there." This is the most basic meaning of the term history.

History also refers to the process of causally related, meaning-laden, unrepeatable events which historical consciousness permits us to perceive, e.g., the history of the American Civil War.[4] Formally, history in this second sense derives from historical consciousness. In practice these two do not exist apart from one another, i.e., there is no historical consciousness without the presence of historical events, and vice versa. As we do not abstractly discover a "meaning" for which we eventually work out a symbol, so there is no historical consciousness which we in time body forth by means of historical events. Or, the one cannot be thought in isolation from the other; the one implies the other. This is why in many situations it does not matter which of these two meanings of the term history is to the fore. Because our consciousness is historical (first definition) we see all of our past and present experience as history (second sense), and we imagine the future events of our personal and social lives as history (second sense).

History in these two senses has existed for three thousand years, i.e., from the formation of Israel. (That there were other, ahistorical types of consciousness also at work in Israel and in Christianity I have no wish to deny; but that is another story.) Drawing upon the work of a great many scholars, I have argued in *History as Myth* that history in the two senses discussed here arises as an integral part of the religious consciousness of the Israelites, and I will return to that to some extent in the succeeding parts of this essay. This means that history arises in intimate association with the symbols and myths which express the religious consciousness of Israel. In this consciousness, and in a modified form in Christianity, history (both senses) is explicitly understood to have its source and guaranty in God.

I wish to elaborate this in a way which I hope will provide a transition to a brief discussion of another sense of the term history, namely history in the sense of modern critical-historical studies; " scientific history," if you prefer.

Myths are stories which are told about symbols. Thus "Yahweh" and "Covenant" were two important symbols of the early Israelites. Around these symbols a story was told of Yahweh's activity from the time of the Creation on man's behalf, including a series of preparatory covenants. Similarly in Christianity, around the symbols of "resurrection" and "cross" a story or myth came to be told, as expressed for example in Paul's sermon in Acts. Myths are already an expression, however limited, of differentiated thought. Of the many potential meanings of the symbols, certain ones are selected and elaborated, e.g., the risen one is "Messiah," he will "return in the last day ," in the meantime he has sent the "Spirit" to us, etc. The myth manifests the will of God explicitly and directly; it is wholly "of God."

The Hebrew, and later Christian, myths had a peculiar quality to them, however. They were open-ended or unfinished myths. Yahweh "goes before" his people; Jesus will "come again." In the meantime one is to be faithful, test the spirits, learn to read the signs of the times, make ready the highway of God, etc. Consequently the ongoing course of human affairs is seen in a sense as an essential extension of the myth and a *further* differentiation of the basic symbols. For example, the advance of the Assyrians upon Israel was not directly and wholly of God. That cruel, destructive advance could not be *simply* identified with the transcendent God of Israel. That it was even an expression of God's chastisement was not immediately obvious, otherwise it would not have had to be proclaimed as such. It was a matter of critical discernment that the advance of the Assyrians was seen in this way, and seen as another episode in the story of Yahweh's dealing with Israel. Moreover, this episode further differentiates the symbol "Yahweh": He is the one who sends the Assyrians to chastise his people.

Thus, because God goes before his people, because he is their future, has promised to sustain them, etc., the ongoing course of experience is understood as significant, purposeful, and creative of meaning, the arena in which again and again the "new thing" which God was doing would be manifested. In short, in the ongoing course of experience history/historical consciousness comes to further expression. This history had its source and guaranty in God; it was an ongoing elaboration of the myth told about the symbols of the community; and because it was an elaboration it was a differentiation of the symbols of the community and of the religious consciousness which found its root expression in those symbols. Moreover, as the prophetic movement demonstrates, this process was increasingly critical as it progressed, i.e., the answer to the question, "What is the will of God?", was seen in an increasingly complex way.

This discussion of the development and differentiation intrinsic to history is pertinent to the third and final definition of history which I wish to present here, namely "history" as scientific history. If history in the first two senses has been with us for three thousand years, this third sense of history emerges clearly only in the eighteenth century. By scientific history I mean the self-consciousness and systematic study of history marked by a rigorously empirical methodology. The emergence of scientific history marks a further and revolutionary differentiation of history (first two senses). The fruits of scientific history have been enormous, and this not least for biblical studies, the history of Christianity, and theology itself.

A full description and analysis of the transition from historical consciousness and history to scientific history would be a lifework. Only a few formal and rather obvious observations are possible here. First, pragmatically at least, the autonomy of scientific history is absolute. Theology can no more interfere in scientific history than it can in genetics. It is a question of methodology, and that is all, and that is that. Second, scientific history is "objective" in the only important sense of that term, i.e., as in any science, there are established and recognized criteria for historical (third sense) argument and judgment which are accepted by all members of the community of scientific historians. This situation in no way impairs their objectivity. The community of scientific historians is made up of all those appropriately trained persons *who accept the presuppositions and methodology of scientific history*. Third, while scientific history is a further differentiation of history/historical consciousness (first and second senses), it is a *differentiation* of that consciousness and history. Scientific history did not spring from the head of Zeus in the seventeenth century, nor was it a repristination of Greek historiography, which was miraculously discovered following a vacuum of 2000 years! Scientific history is a methodological isolation of a *portion* of historical consciousness/history, viz., the empirical. Moreover, let it be said loudly and clearly that the scientific historian is usually unaware of and often hostilely indifferent to (sic) the relationship between scientific history and the two previous definitions of history. That is his problem and perhaps his loss in the long run, but it does not make much difference in the short run. Fourth, and closely related to our third point, what the scientific historian is usually (there *are* exceptions) unaware of without immediate loss is that scientific history *is* a differentiation of history (first two senses), and that this history (first two senses) provides him with his essential and unexamined presuppositions. Moreover, it is history (first two senses) which has provided the possibility of the *methodology* of scientific history. This possibility was established by the biblical myth which denied the archaic notion that the ongoing course of experience is the immediate expression and of the sacred, which affirmed the transcendence of God and thereby enabled man to place some "distance" between himself and what he experienced. It was part of the point of our earlier discussion of the process of differentiation in history (first two senses) to show how the differentiation happily effected by scientific history was not without significant preparation. Fifth, and finally, when scientific history ceases to see itself as a methodology and proclaims implicitly or explicitly that its methodologically delimited area of inquiry is exhaustive of historical reality, then you have "historicism," and the beginning of the end of the *total* historical enterprise . Scientific history exists as a secondary abstraction within the larger body of historical consciousness/history.

This is the best distinction I am able to make at the present time between (1) historical consciousness, (2) events as perceived by historical consciousness, and (3) scientific history. I turn now to a discussion of myth in preparation for a fuller discussion of the relationship between myth and history in the latter part of this paper.

II. HOW SHALL WE UNDERSTAND MYTH?

First, a very elementary observation. When I speak of myth I do not have in mind "mythological stories," as we find, for example, in various anthologies of stories of the activities and escapades of the divinities of Greece and Rome. These stories, while ultimately deriving from myth, had already become trivialized and made a matter of literature in the Hellenistic period. In mythological stories the multivalent, overdetermined, and hence mysterious and life-enhancing qualities of the symbols in the myth, are drastically reduced. The characteristics and areas of activity of the respective gods are relatively determined. A further degradation takes place when the mythological story comes to have a "point," or worse yet, is allegorized. The richness and mystery of the myth and its symbols are thus trivialized and lost, as is its power to cosmicize or legitimize the world. Or, more accurately and more complexly, it is probably the decline in the power of the myth to articulate human experience which gives rise to mythological stories, which stories in turn reinforce the loss of the power of the myth, etc. In any case the power of the myth is destroyed, the gods are "dead." (There then only remains a self-conscious demythologization and scepticism — and the emergence of new myths!) It is not mythological stories with which we are concerned here, however.[5]

I understand myth to be made up of symbols and sets of symbols woven into a dramatic-ritual and narrative form. The symbols, including the general linguistic context in which the symbols are set, are amazingly complex and rich. On the one hand a symbol or set of symbols gives a particular direction to thought, e.g., an archaic direction, an eschatological direction, a movement toward the *restitutio in integrum* of Indian thought, etc. In this sense they exclude certain possibilities of perceiving experience. On the other hand, within the limits set in this way the symbols are multivalent or "overdetermined," giving them the ability to evoke a practically infinite number of interpretations and developments in many media, including the forms which are used to structure daily life. The basic symbols are always concrete; and they are usually, if not always, body or body-related symbols, e.g., earth, food, blood, sex, house, death, life, etc.

The fundamental function of myth, it still needs to be said, is not primarily etiological. Rather, the fundamental function is one of cosmicization; of giving meaning and shape to the world; of stating what is really real, self-founded, true, and good. Only through myth is there created in the spirit of man "a special conception of the cosmos; only through this act is cosmos, an apprehended world, a world that is homely and houselike, man's dwelling in the world, made possible again and again."[6] Because the myth speaks authoritatively of the real and the true, it perforce speaks of the sacred. In all of this I am obviously indebted to Mircea Eliade.

What I have said up to this point is widely, although not universally, accepted; and is relatively uncontroversial. The next step which I want to take is more controversial. It is this: The only perception of reality which is possible is ultimately that which comes to us by means of the symbol structure called "language," and it is the language of myth which at the most fundamental level enables us to perceive reality. In the case of the archaic mentality the participation in myth and the associated perception of experience is immediate and largely uncritical. However, in the differentiated consciousness, preeminently that of modern Western man, man's participation and perception is non-immediate and critical. Myth is now "broken," i.e., myth is believed as myth.[7] In *both* cases, however, there is no way around myth and language. Myth may be criticized, its inadequacies recognized, modified, or replaced by other myths; but we cannot move around or behind myth. We can only move through myth; and our lifelong and never completed task is to move into the incredible richness of myth, the symbols of which it speaks, and the thought to which it gives rise. Thus, in any area of inquiry, after we have exercised the most rigorous and fruitful dialectic or entered most deeply into the "hermeneutics of suspicion" (Ricoeur), we are, at the end, in my judgment, forced to recognize that the mythic-linguistic "given" with which we started still remains as the given, the foundation of all our intellectual and practical activity. What Collingwood says in the following quotation concerning "religion" and "religious consciousness" is even more applicable to "myth" and "mythic consciousness." Although it was written a generation ago, it sums up nicely what I have been saying in this section:

> To fancy that religion lives either below or above the limits of reflective thought is fatally to misconceive either the nature of religion or the nature of reflective thought. It would be nearer the truth to say that in religion the life of reflection is concentrated in its intensest form, and that the special problems of theoretical and practical life all take their special forms by segregation out of the body of the religious consciousness, and retain their vitality so far as they preserve their connection with it and with each other in it.[8]

III. THE CONTINUING VALIDITY AND PERVASIVENESS OF MYTH

Some of those who reflect upon the nature of myth wish to restrict that term to *archaic* myth, that is, to those myths which provide the *unchanging* archetype of all human activities, which understand the sacred to be manifested directly and relatively unambiguously in immediate experience, in which the believer participates in an immediate and largely uncritical way, etc. If "myth" is defined in this way, then clearly it follows *by definition* that much of biblical experience and most of contemporary experience is non-mythic, and that myth and the reflection upon myth is at best of peripheral importance to contemporary experience and reflection — theological, historical, social, or whatever.

In my judgment, however, to define myth in this restricted way is arbitrary and misleading. It is arbitrary because it takes *one form* (granted, the oldest form) of myth and declares that to be the totality of myth. It is misleading because it prevents us from perceiving the continuingly important role of myth in our experience and reflection. In this position it is asserted that whereas once it was necessary for men to use the symbolic narratives of myths in order to relate human experience to its transcendent referent or ultimate meaning (the process of cosmicization), today we may cosmicize our world apart from myth. In response to such a position I am led to the following questions and observations.

First, one is led to ask: How then does man cosmicize his world apart from myth? Perhaps the best answer to that question is to say, variously, that human experience is self-explanatory, that it does not need any explanation, that one should not raise such questions because there are no answers, etc. In terms of an immediate pragmatism, that genre of answer is unbeatable! One declares oneself the winner, and withdraws! The stark inadequacies of this type of answer are, on the other hand, so obvious as not to need review here.

Second, to the Christian who would claim that his faith is not mythic, or no longer mythic in any significant sense, then I am puzzled indeed. One can speak of creation, fall, messiah, resurrection, "This is my body, given for you," judgment, divine law, and much, much more in a similar vein, and yet say that myth is not important for Christian faith?! True, this is not archaic myth, and it is for us "broken myth"; but it is for us *functionally* precisely what it was for archaic man: an indispensable symbol-set out of which is evolved a world-view, or series of related world-views, which make an ultimately important although logically non-demonstrable truth claim. Or, in both cases, the myth serves to cosmicize the world. If myth is not present in Christianity, then "something else" is present which has exactly the same basic function!

Third, and somewhat related to the preceding paragraph, I am puzzled as to where Christian theologians see the substance of their faith and discipline arising, if not from myth and its symbols. Out of philosophical statements or systems? Out of empirical historical facts? However useful philosophy and critical historical studies may be in criticizing, clarifying, or supporting religion and theology, surely it is not the substance of those activities. More plausibly it might be said that while myth does give rise to reflective thought, theological and otherwise, nevertheless, as a result of sustained cognitive development, the mythic foundation of theology becomes increasingly unimportant, or even of only negative significance. This too fails, it seems to me. Theological reflection continues to be, no matter how abstruse, concerned with such matters as Jesus the Christ, continues to return to and be empowered by those symbols, and would have nothing to reflect upon apart from those symbols and the life of the community which is informed by them.

Such intellectualist derogations of the role of myth in religion and theology seem to fail in at least two specific ways. It is not recognized to what extent all language is symbolic and hence multivalent and equivocal. (The attraction of mathematical logic is to try to arrive at a *symbolic* language which has, however, only one meaning for each symbol, and hence is univocal.) Further, it is not recognized how the power of myth continues to surge through such seemingly neutral words, as, for example, "future" and "body." Thus the significance of "future" and "body" is quite different for the traditional Hindu theologian and the Christian theologian because these terms arise respectively out of and continue to carry the power of different myths.

Further, the intellectualist derogation of myth fails to recognize that only in myth can the necessarily non-objective character of our talk of God or the sacred come to adequate expression. Only in the indeterminate, multivalent expressions of myth can the mystery of God be adequately expressed. It is the relatively determined and univocal and objectified statements of discursive language about God which makes them of limited and temporary value. Theological systems come and go without permanent damage to (and often to the renewal of!) Christian faith; the biblical myth or myths remain as long as Christian faith remains. In the words of Dupré:

> The myth possesses two qualities which make it irreplaceable for the religious symbolization process. One is a capacity to reflect, without objectivating the reality upon which it reflects. Earlier we saw that all religious symbols are reflective as well as nonobjective. We now may add that outside the myth such symbols cannot be formed and, once they exist, cannot be properly understood. This quality of myth is but a result of its unique ability to reconcile and integrate opposed facets of existence.[9]

It is a consequence of this situation that even so philosophical and discursive a theologian as Bernard Lonergan, while he has many minimizing statements to make about myth,[10] must also indirectly and even directly affirm its continuing validity.[11]

It is along such lines as these, then, that I would argue for the continuing necessity and viability of myth in our culture. If this position is somewhat controversial, then the next step which I would like to take is much more so. It is this: The essential character and direction of our personal and social lives are shaped by myth; or, it is the power of particular myths which determine, by way of determining our fundamental presuppositions, the way in which we shape our cultural, social, political, and economic lives. We do nothing of significance which is not informed by myth in a fundamental way; and the more significant our act, the more this is true. It is the symbols within the context of the myth which give rise to all thought.

The particular myth or myths which inform a particular activity or attitude will vary of course, and just what are the operative myth(s) must be determined in each case. However, I would maintain that any culture which possesses any effective degree of coherence has one myth or selected set of myths which supplies the *dominant* mythic structure for that society.[12] This is not to deny that other non-dominant myths are present and effective to some degree. Indeed, they probably always are in post-archaic cultures, and these non-dominant myths may even be themselves dominant among a certain limited number of individuals. Nevertheless, in a reasonably well-integrated culture one myth or set of myths will dominate, controlling other myths. Thus, in terms of Ricoeur's analysis in Chapter Five of *The Symbolism of Evil*, the "Adamic myth" and the "myth of the exiled soul" cannot both be equally effective in a given culture, at a given time. As far as these two particular myths are concerned, in the West it is the biblical Adamic myth which dominates, in spite of the presence, and even *necessary* presence according to Ricoeur, of the counter-myths. It is this dominance, of which in the West the Adamic myth is only a part, which gives homogeneity to a culture, and makes other cultures seem like "far lands." It is this situation which leads Raymond Panikkar to say that if Christianity and its culture and Hinduism (which cannot be conceived of apart from its culture) are to be brought into any fruitful relationship, then a process of *trans*mythologization must take place. It only needs to be added here, as is implicit in what I have said above, that in my judgment it is the *dominant* myths of the Bible (e.g., the good creation, the Adamic myth, promised land, Messiah, and eschatological [not apocalyptic] fulfillment) which still supply the dominant mythic structures of the West; and which give the West the definite homogeneity which, in spite of everything, it still possesses, i.e., the commitment to the concrete, the pragmatic, to history, and man's responsibility for history, to the future, etc.

IV. THE RELATIONSHIP OF MYTH AND HISTORY

Some might claim that the position which I have sketched here in regard to myth could lead to some kind of "mythomania." In my judgment, this is not the case, however. As I have stated, myth is for us *broken* myth, and it will always remain so. Short of the total collapse of our culture, there is no possibility of our returning to the state of original participation (Barfield) or a first naïveté (Ricoeur). To say that myth and symbol give rise to and form the horizon of thought does not denigrate thought. *Both* are essential, that is the point. It is myth and symbol which give rise to our fundamental presuppositions, our cosmos, our particular subjectivity. It is the sovereign role of critical thought to differentiate out of this subjectivity various areas of specialized inquiry. As we discussed earlier, critical consciousness itself is one such differentiation out of the dominant myths and symbols of Western civilization. This is one kind of thought to which our myths and symbols give rise; this is one way in which we have tutored our subjectivity in the West. In this process of tutoring, a specific and sophisticated methodology has arisen, namely that of the practicing scientific historian. (And, in a less formal and disciplined way, most or all of us are "practicing historians," i.e., most or all of us participate in modern, critical historical consciousness.) The methodology and the fruit of the methodology which arise from this tutoring of our subjectivity is quite "objective" or "public," i.e., it is shared and can be appealed to in agreed upon ways by those within the community who have tutored their subjectivity in this way. The myths and symbols upon which this methodology is based have nothing *directly* to say about how the details of this methodology are worked out, and most emphatically they have nothing to say about how or to what areas the methodology is applied. Scientific history may legitimately be used to call into question or "attack" the successive differentiations of historical consciousness which arose out of the primary biblical symbols. This attack may take the form of demonstrating that certain differentiations of consciousness, e.g., those influenced by Hellenistic philosophy, are distortive of or not exhaustive of the meaning of the biblical symbols — as has sometimes been claimed. More radically, the impact of the past century of scientific historical studies of Scripture and religious traditions has been an "attack" upon any literalistic differentiation of historical consciousness out of the biblical symbols. Or, better perhaps, scientific history has helped and forced us to a clearer differentiation between the various elements of Scripture and tradition, e.g., empirical, legendary, poetic, redactional, etc. Even further, scientific history together with philosophical, theological, and other kinds of reflection upon the results of scientific history, have enabled us once more to perceive symbol as symbol, to see symbol as exploratory rather than explanatory. In part this process has been one of restoration; a restoration of the exploratory, overdetermined quality which symbol possessed in pre-rationalistic, pre-scientific culture. In part this process brought about a new differentiation of historical consciousness, for to perceive symbol as symbol, as exploratory, in a post-scientific culture is more than restoration. Symbols look different *now*; symbol is now more clearly differentiated from other aspects of consciousness. However, what scientific history cannot do is to attack or destroy the symbol itself, in distinction from the differentiations out of the symbol itself. Scientific history cannot destroy the symbol itself because such an effort lies outside of the methodology, and hence outside of the capability, of scientific history. If it were "somehow" to destroy the symbols out of which historical consciousness, history, and scientific history arose, then this would be a process of self-destruction for scientific history.

So, with the aid of hindsight, we understand that the "attack" of scientific history was not exactly what it was often thought to be. It was a *prophetic* attack, i.e., one not designed to utterly destroy the mythic tradition, but to criticize, cleanse, and reappropriate that tradition. As in the case of the Hebrew prophets, it was an attack upon the tradition with the help of and in the name of the tradition. And, again as in the situation of the Hebrew prophets, the symbols and myths of the tradition had within them the potential for this attack, a potential which was realized as those myths and symbols gave rise to thought in the ongoing historical process. Specifically, in the case of scientific historical methodology, we would want to point by way of example to two particular ideas carried in biblical myths and symbols which inform historical methodology. These are, first, the sovereign rule of a transcendent God; and, second, that fulfillment (the Kingdom of God) lies in the future, not in the past, e.g., not in the restoration of a "lost Paradise" or some other paradigmatic moment. These ideas, so foreign to the archaic societies out of which the Hebrew people arose, are ingredient to the Hebrew's historical appropriation of experience.

These two fundamental ideas become reflectively and systematically spelled out with the arising of modern, critical historical thought, and issue respectively in two fundamental points in historical methodology: the refusal to absolutize any human creation, and the refusal to find unchanging criteria in any given period or culture of the past. Consequently, it was inevitable that historical studies would come to criticize any and every tendency of Christian tradition to absolutize its symbols and myths, even those found in Scripture. Or, it was inevitable that myth should come to be "broken" within the biblical tradition because of the character of that very tradition itself; indeed, the process of the breaking of myth has already begun in the Bible. It was the function of critical historical studies to make the critique which led to the self-conscious and thoroughgoing "breaking" of myth. This was done, in the "prophetic tradition," with the help of and in the name of the (historical) tradition of which it was a part. Thus, the two centuries and more of struggle between Christian theology and critical historical studies has been a family quarrel in which all sides have benefited in terms of greater self-understanding. Critical historical studies had the strength to do this because, although it was differentiated out of the much less self-conscious and systematic historical understanding of biblical traditions, nevertheless it had acquired a real independence in the process of differentiation. This independence was strong enough that it could stand against the reluctance of conservative Christian thinking to submit its symbols and myths to the systematic, reflective, historical thought which was arising out of those very symbols and myths.

One criticism or challenge to Christian trâdition which historical studies could not make, however, was to call into question the validity of the historical perception of reality *per se*. (Other civilizations have challenged this, and increasingly voices within our own civilization have made this challenge; but that is another matter.) Historical studies could not make this challenge in a serious way without it resulting in, first, the end of historical studies, and, second, the turning of a family quarrel into a confrontation between completely divergent worldviews and presuppositions. In other words, the symbols and myths which bring a historical view of experience to expression give rise to a dynamic which is capable of infinite self-criticism, including that which is manifested in the discipline of history; but this dynamic of self-criticism cannot be turned in an absolute or radical way against the symbols and myths themselves without turning cosmos into chaos and thus destroying the entire enterprise of history.[13]

V. Conclusion

At the beginning of this paper I indicated that in examining myth and the crisis of historical consciousness my fundamental concern is with the *crisis* of historical consciousness. As a Christian and as a critical-conservative participant in Western spirituality, I wish to retain historical consciousness both for myself and for my culture. As I have indicated, the attacks upon historical consciousness are diverse and powerful, including such formidable figures as Lévi-Strauss, Mircea Eliade, and B. F. Skinner. In a different vein, but with much in common with these attacks, are such pervasive social phenomena as the drug culture, astrology, much science fiction, various religious and quasi-religious cults emphasizing enthusiasm and the "mystic now" (the Jesus people and some rock music are in this category), the general anti-historical bias in much of the counter-culture and not-so-counter culture, etc. Nathan Scott has recently described phenomena of this kind, particularly in their literary dimension, in rich detail in "The Landscape of Contemporary Apocalypse."[14] He has correctly characterized these diverse anti-historical forces as "apocalyptic." They find the "radically demanding historical hour" intolerable and look "toward the time when time no more shall be."[15] This loss of the courage to be in history is the result of vast numbers of persons finding that experience is increasingly unmanageable in historical terms; that increasingly history is experienced as terror.

This anti-historical movement is obviously highly complex. As I experience it I share Scott's indignation with it and its excesses. At the same time, although with some greater effort, I can experience compassion in relation to those who find themselves caught up in the terror of history. This compassion leads us, leads me at least, to work toward a situation in which we once again have the courage to accept the "radically demanding historical hour." This work must be done a few small steps at a time, and what is suggested in this paper are a few, small steps in the area of our reflection upon and our appropriation of historical consciousness.

I do not think that the failure of so many to be willing to face the admittedly great demands of a historical appropriation of experience can be laid entirely to an "ill will' or "an evil spirit" in our culture, for this is as much a result as a cause of our inclination to the diverse forms of "apocalyptic." The apocalyptic thrust in our culture is in part a legitimate protest against the way in which we have come to understand and to act out of our historical consciousness.

More specifically, the protest is right in rejecting the too abstract, rationalistic, and narrow way in which we appreciate and utilize our historical consciousness. There is an arrogance in the way many historians preen themselves on the narrowness of their understanding of the scope of historical reflection. There goes with this, ironically, the pretense by historians to know clearly more than it is possible to know clearly, even within the restricted realm which historians (lay and professional) take to be peculiarly theirs. This questionable claim to "clarity" arises out of the historian's highly touted specialization, for it is just this which excludes many dimensions of experience; dimensions of experience which have in fact an effect upon the phenomena being studied by the historian. Or, "clarity" is achieved at the price of abstraction. Another way of expressing this is to point out that the typical exercise of historical consciousness by the professional historian and others, has a very inadequate perception of the "limits" which we encounter in experience, and the mystery which is experienced when we encounter those limits. It is this abstraction, so characteristic of our prevailing appreciation of history, which renders it a "terror," and this situation is intuited by those who are drawn toward apocalyptic. (Let me say parenthetically, in the interest of averting misunderstanding, that the professional historian must continue, in many situations, with his abstract and specialized inquiries; but he should place these in a larger context, and hence become more modest about the scope of his claims.)

As a few small steps toward meeting this partially legitimate protest, I have two intimately related suggestions to make. The first suggestion is that we cease to reify history (all three senses) as a description of experience which is self-evidently true, and which in its explicit observations and judgments is complete and exhaustive. My second suggestion is that we become aware of the ground of history, and that we permit this awareness to permeate our historical consciousness, not by changing the particular results or applications of that consciousness, but by placing the whole historical enterprise within a different and wider horizon. I wish to develop each of these in turn.

First, then, I want to urge that we cease reifying history as a self-explanatory and self-evidently true and supremely privileged form of knowledge. The study of archaic civilizations and the philosophical reflection coming out of that study (e.g., Lévi-Strauss) have made impossible the continued reification of history (especially in our third sense). Moreover, it is the abstractness of this rationalistic view of history which is so characteristic of the malaise of our prevalent Western spirituality with its arrogant insistence upon the clear and distinct idea at every point (in McLuhan's phrase, "everything in its place, a place for everything"), with its total orientation to control (our increasingly less passionate *and* more destructive wars, as Goodman observes), with its closed attitude to mystery, etc.

It is this spirituality which has unleashed the terror of history and brought about our contemporary "chaos" manifested so vividly in the theater of the absurd, the grotesque in the visual arts, the cacophony of much contemporary music, and the diverse realm of apocalyptic of which Nathan Scott speaks. These ambiguous developments, so heavy with portent for both good *and* evil, seem to indicate that the human spirit cannot tolerate the abstraction and restrictiveness of modern Western spirituality of which the conventional view of history is a part.

The corrective to all this as far as the realm of historical consciousness and reflection is concerned is the full and open admission of the mythic dimension in our concept of history. Such a program would not be a mythomania, and it would in no way threaten the "objectivity" and importance of critical historical studies. It would not threaten even the most reductionistic of these studies, *except* insofar as such studies make the ahistorical claim to present a full and exhaustive account of experience. In other words, what I am advocating is not any kind of nostalgic "going back," but rather a post-critical position in which we accept fully the results and continuing validity of critical historical studies, and then go on to recognize that these studies are not exactly what they thought themselves to be. They would be placed in a larger context. Just as we have come to understand myth as myth, so we have to be able to understand history *as* history. Myth understood or believed *as* myth can, of course, be taken in all seriousness, be recognized as an important source of truth, and even be accepted as articulating for an individual or community an ultimate worldview or faith stance; but it cannot be understood as literally or factually true, self-evidently exhaustive of all meaning, etc. Similarly, history understood or believed as history could be accepted in all seriousness as an important source of truth, and even be accepted as articulating an individual's or community's ultimate worldview. (I myself would so accept it.) At the same time, however, it would not be possible to reify history, proclaiming it as "factual," as self-evidently true, self-explanatory, exhaustive of all possible meaning, etc. Or, history like myth is a "language game," with all of the possibilities and limitations which attach to that status. This would further the possibility of a dialogue of civilizations, a possibility which has up to now been explored in a very fragmentary way because of the exaggerated claims of an inadequately understood historical consciousness.

The acceptance of such an approach to history would be shattering to the dominant modern Western spirituality, as was our coming to accept myth as myth. The acceptance of myth as myth was, on the one hand, shattering to many because it made us very aware that we could not accept myth as literal, as explanatory in an empirical sense, as being located in the space and time made familiar by geography and calendars. On the other hand, this development grew out of and supported the dominant Western spirituality oriented to suspicion, the "clear and distinct idea," analysis, control, etc. The acceptance of myth as myth also had another, largely unrecognized,[16] and ultimately more significant effect. In taking away the misunderstanding of myth as literal and empirically explanatory which had evolved in the West, it prepared the way for a new appropriation (in part a reappropriation) of myth as linguistic event, as cosmogenic or world-shaping, as exploratory, etc. This in turn has enabled us to see the mythic dimension of component in all human activity and reflection, including that reflection called "history." Thus, we took an uncritical acceptance of myth into the modern, critical age; we found it unacceptable and therefore rejected it; but now we are in a position to recognize myth as having been operative all along, investing even such supposed "objective" disciplines as historical studies. This is shattering because things are not the way we thought they were.

The result is to deny the dominant Western spirituality oriented to analysis and control insofar as it claims to be exhaustive of what it means to know. It is, on the other hand, and more significantly, to reclaim that spirituality by freeing it from its restrictiveness, placing it within a larger context and uniting it with its mythic origins. This is to arrive at a place and to know it for the first time (Eliot); it is a recovery of tradition.

This new situation seems to raise a problem for some persons. They maintain: Just as the recognition of myth as myth meant the end of myth as a means of forming and empowering man, so the recognition of history as history would mean the end of history as a convincing way of actualizing personal and social existence, and empowering us to act in a historical way. This argument seems to say that we must be "true believers" in Eric Hoffer's sense (absolutist and closed), or not "believers" at all. I cannot agree that this exhausts our options. Rather, history like myth is seen to be the linguistic production of human subjectivity and as such it cannot be claimed to be "objective," i.e., absolutely true, beyond suspicion or change, exhaustive of reality. The Christian myth and history are intimately related although not identical ways of tutoring our subjectivity in order to apprehend and act in the world in a distinctive and creative way. *Within* the community of those who have tutored their subjectivity in this way there is ample room (indeed, it is demanded) for "objective" talk of theology or of history. This does not mean, however, that we must or can forget the faith dimension of the theological or historical enterprise; that both involve a "wager" as to their being the most fruitful way in which to apprehend experience. Moreover, because we recognize the practically infinite multivalency of our own symbols, we cannot be closed to having our apprehension of our own symbols enriched and criticized by other religions and cultures. John Dunne speaks of this process as a "passing over," and Raymond Panikkar speaks of it as "transmythologization." This is, admittedly, a "risky" enterprise; but then faith has always been a risky enterprise. The "true believer" "eliminates" risk by absolutely rejecting all other positions; the sceptic "eliminates" risk by rejecting all positions (except the alogical position of scepticism; why not be sceptical of your own scepticism?). There is a third option of risk and openness which is expressed when we *affirm* myth as myth, and history as history.

The accepting of history as history cannot, as I have implied, be taken without our becoming aware of the ground of history and permitting this awareness to permeate our historical consciousness.[17] I have argued here and elsewhere that this ground is the mythic images arising out of biblical experience, that history "has its source and finds its guaranty and support in God." Our modern, critical perception of history has been differentiated out of those images, or, those images gave rise to that thought, that perception of experience which today we call "history." This differentiation was *inevitable*, and the benefits which accrued are too obvious to need review here. At the same time there was the loss which we have discussed, the reifying of history, and the assumption that it is the self-evidently true and privileged form of knowledge.

It is against this latter misleading development that the various expressions of the rejection of historical consciousness have arisen. If we are at least to put the "house of history" in defensible intellectual order, if we are to save the "house of history" for our civilization, and if we are to enter into a dialogue of civilizations, then we must let the mythic origins of history permeate our historical consciousness. Perhaps the various protests against the imperialism of modern historical consciousness will force this permeation.

Myth is the linguistic means whereby our consciousness is expanded and our experience given form and order; a means whereby our world is cosmicized, the "appearances are saved." The set of myths in which historical consciousness comes to expression is a *particular* way in which consciousness is expanded, the appearances are saved, and the self is shaped. This involves, of course, speaking of such matters as first cause, final end, ultimate meaning, etc. The biblical myths speak *explicitly* of these matters; modern historical consciousness (third sense) obviously and properly does not speak *explicitly* of this dimension of experience. Nevertheless, this dimension of experience is present in historical experience and the systematic reflection upon it. This is obvious because history is not perceived as chaos, but as manifesting order and meaning. This order and meaning is, however, *implicitly* present in our differentiated modern experience of history. *Implicitly* historical experience is intrinsically meaningful (structured); it has "origins" ("beginnings"); and "results" ("ends"). Partial meanings are *implicitly* understood as parts of a larger all-encompassing "final" meaning. Without this implicit larger schema historical experience would not be possible. Myth has given rise to and continues to operate within our modern sense of history; it makes historical time possible; it is the continuing source of that consciousness-expanding, appearance-saving construct called "history." Myth permeates our historical sense, and becoming self-conscious about this already existing situation is the way toward achieving the goal of letting our historical sense be permeated by the ground of history.

The self-conscious recognition of this mythic dimension of history would balance, complete, and deepen our sense of what it means to be in history (all three senses). It is widely recognized and often explicitly stated that in history the self comes to be understood in terms of the self, i.e., in terms of what the self has made within the realm of history. To this there needs to be added the recognition of the mythic dimension of history; the recognition that implicit within our historical consciousness is a "limit." In history the self stands before and is dependent upon its "limit," i.e., the "beginning" and "end" (or "ground") of which history does not speak explicitly (as do the myths). This is the limit, the mystery, the darkness before which scientific history stands, and of which in all modesty it will not speak, except insofar as it does so implicitly in speaking about the self in terms of itself.

If we were to come to the recognition of this situation there would be a depth to our sense of history which would bring to an end the reification of historical fact, the imperialism of the claims of history to be the exhaustive and supremely privileged form of knowledge, and the rationalistic abstractness which provokes the protests of the various forms of contemporary apocalyptic.

In this way there could be a recovery of historical consciousness which would once again demonstrate its validity in terms of comprehensiveness and fruitfulness.

NOTES

[1]Cf. Van A. Harvey, *The Historian and the Believer* (New York: The Macmillan Co., 1966). Cf. also T. A. Robert's review article of Harvey's book found in *Religious Studies*, VII: 251-57.

[2]Paul Ricoeur, *Freud and Philosophy: An Essay on Interpretation* (New Haven: Yale University Press, 1970), p. 31.

[3]Ricoeur, *Freud and Philosophy*, p. 551.

[4]Of course, there is the further trivial sense of "history" where it means a "book," e.g., Smith's *History of the American Civil War*.

[5]In reference to this distinction between "mythology" and "myth," Louis Dupré makes a similar distinction between "demythologizing," which is affirmed, and "demythizing," which is "ultimately destructive of the particular nature of religious symbols." Louis Dupré, *The Other Dimension* (New York: Doubleday, 1972), p. 277. Richard A. Ray suggests, and I agree, that turning myth into mythological story "involves the Western attempt to escape the power of myth itself in our own lives" (letter of July 2, 1973). Cf. Lee W. Gibbs, "Myth and the Mystery of the Future," collected in this volume, for further discussion of these terms.

[6]Martin Buber, *I and Thou* (New York: Charles Scribner's Sons, 1958), p. 54.

[7]Cf. George Weckman, "Believing Myth as Myth," collected in this volume, for further discussion of this point.

[8]R. G. Collingwood, *The Idea of History* (London: Oxford University Press, 1946), p. 315.

[9]Louis Dupré, *The Other Dimension*, p. 273.

[10]Cf. Bernard J. F. Lonergan, S.J., *Method in Theology* (New York: Herder and Herder, 1972), pp. 8, 28, 92-93, 98, 213, 306.

[11]Cf. Lonergan, *Method in Theology*, pp. 58-59, 60-61, 85.

[12]I would argue that certain biblical symbols and myths, e.g., the Adamic myth, still constitute the dominant symbols and myths in Western civilization. I am, of course, aware, given the social chaos of the West today, that this matter is debatable.

[13]It is just this which has taken place, usually surreptitiously, in those historians who pursue a thorough-going, nihilistic relativism: nihilism=chaos.

[14]Nathan A. Scott, Jr., "The Landscape of Contemporary Apocalypse," *The Journal of Religion* (1973): 1-35.

[15]*Ibid.*, 34.

[16]Giambattista Vico (1668-1744) recognized this in part.

[17]Lévi-Strauss has taken the first step without showing any inclination to take the second. But then he has no interest in retaining our Western historical consciousness, preferring to replace it with something altogether different. For a provocative statement of the limitations of Lévi-Strauss see Paul Ricoeur, *The Conflict of Interpretations: Essays in Hermeneutics*, ed. Don Ihde (Evanston: Northwestern University Press, 1974), pp. 3-96.

Myth and the Mystery of the Future

Lee W. Gibbs

T HE theme "Myth and the Crisis of Historical Consciousness" brings into sharp focus the tension between "myth" and "history." These two concepts have been set in radical opposition to each other by many recent theologians, philosophers of religion, and historians of religion. My essay is committed to the view that there is nothing inherently necessary or final in the apparent crisis which the confrontation of myth and history has caused for so many Jewish and Christian believers, and that a critical reevaluation of the mythic mode of perception, expression, and communication may help to overcome the crisis, whether that crisis be personal or theological.

Part I of my paper is an analysis of modern historical consciousness and of the crisis which has arisen for that particular form of consciousness. This crisis is at least partially responsible for the revival of interest in the reality and function of myth. Part II argues that the future ultimately lies beyond the grasp of man's knowledge, prediction, and control, thereby producing in many persons a profound and disturbing sense of dread and fascination through their confrontation with that which is unknown. The only appropriate mode of expressing and communicating the consequent experience of transcendent mystery, it is argued, is through the imaginatively intuited symbolic images embodied in myth. Part III then sets forth a reassertion of the mythical depiction of the future in Judaism and Christianity. I believe these Jewish and Christian myths still possess the inherent power to convert the time process from meaningless repetition and absurdity into a cosmic drama in which men may find meaning, purpose, and value through their own existential involvement and participation.

I. The Contemporary Crisis of Historical Consciousness

Our modern historical consciousness has made us all aware of the fact that every historical era has its own characteristic general assumptions or presuppositions which are usually hidden from the view of the majority of those who look through them like spectacles at the world and at the problems raised by human existence. It has been widely recognized that the two fundamental presuppositions of modern Western civilization are science and history.[1] Space does not allow for a careful exposition of the origins and characteristics of these two basic presuppositions of the modern *Weltanschauung*; this task has been pursued extensively and often enough elsewhere. Suffice it to say that ancient and medieval intellectuals knew quite a bit about science, just as history was known and written before the eighteenth century. What is at issue here is basically a question of perspective and of scientific attitudes and methods. The modern empirical study of nature has revolutionized the world and re-created the mind of modern man both by its methods and by its technological applications. The application of the empirical methods of science to the study of man — not only as a biological organism but also to human history, civilization, social organization, and so forth — led to the liberation of history and the other social sciences (*Geisteswissenschaften*) as empirical disciplines independent from philosophy.

Although history as an empirical discipline is restricted by definition and methodology to a study of the *human past*, its revolutionary impact on modern consciousness reaches far beyond a better and clearer understanding of man's history. For modern Western man at least, human consciousness has itself become "historical." Perhaps the most decisive result of the modern study of history upon human thought is the emphasis upon the conception of real change in history, of a real evolution in the condition and thought of the human race.[2] The consequent relativism which inevitably accompanies such a conception of real change, and which is so characteristic of modern historical consciousness, has been admirably described by Carl Becker:

> What is peculiar to the modern mind is the disposition and the determination to regard ideas and concepts, the truth of things as well as the things themselves, as changing entities, the character and significance of which at any given time can be fully grasped only by regarding them as points in an endless process of differentiation, of unfolding, of waste, and repair. . . . Historical mindedness is so much a preoccupation of modern thought that we can identify a particular thing only by pointing to the various things it successively was before it came to be that particular thing which it will presently cease to be.[3]

When historical consciousness asserts itself in terms of a fully self-conscious metaphysics or ontology, the nature of reality itself is said to be historical. The key for understanding the ultimate mysteries of the universe and of man's origins, existence, and destiny, is to be sought only in the history of man and human civilization. Man is understood to be a historical, temporal being who is consciously determined and limited in the present both by the human and also by his own personal past; yet this historically conditioned man still remains open in his freedom to assume responsibility for making or creating history through his openness to the future. The evolutionary process, which has heretofore been unconscious, now becomes in man conscious and voluntary; man can now freely and creatively begin to direct and shape the course of history through responsible decisions grounded in his understanding of the historical process. Although there is often a strong dualistic tendency to differentiate history as the realm of freedom, spontaneity, creativity, and novelty as over against the closed, deterministic, endlessly repetitive system of cause and effect in the realm of nature, a thorough-going metaphysics or ontology of history extends the category of history even to the universe and nature. In other words, the historical categories of "event," "novelty," and "development" are analogically applied to the understanding of nature as history.[4]

The historical mode of modern consciousness is now being called into question by challenges emerging on at least two different fronts. The first front is emerging within the camp of those who hold the historical perspective on reality — namely, from those who are experiencing what Mircea Eliade has called "the terror of history."[5] This experience of horror has occurred in persons suffering from various degrees of historical relativism and "future shock," both of which may lead in their most acute forms to a nihilistic feeling of the chaotic senselessness and purposelessness of human existence.

The paradox of historical consciousness is that the more historically-minded one becomes, the fewer defenses are left for fortifying oneself against the terror of history. Without some kind of trans-historical or meta-historical frame of reference and meaning, it becomes more and more difficult to make sense of and therefore to endure the pressures emanating from the catastrophes and horrors of history. The more modern a man becomes, the less chance he has of freely making or creating history.[6] The most staggering of all the blows leading to the overwhelming vertigo of an ultimately self-defeating historical relativism is the final recognition of the relativity of the modern awareness of historical relativity itself. Historical relativity leads many persons to the arid spiritual wasteland of nihilism, of a despairing philosophy spelling the paralysis of intellectual and spiritual powers because of an inescapable feeling of the absurdity of existence. The only viable options open to one who finds himself in such a state of existential despair and hopelessness lie in the directions of committing suicide, of incongruously and defiantly affirming the meaning and value of human existence in spite of the evident absurdity of the universe, or of finding some other way to fill the spiritual vacuum.

The second front from which an attack is being launched against "the tyranny of modern historical consciousness" has arisen within the circle of heterogeneous movements lumped together under the name of "the counter-culture." The counter-culture is calling into question both the conventional scientific world-view (along with the "technocratic" or "super-industrial" society which is founded upon it) *and* the conventional interpretation of reality and the being of man as historical in nature. The movement away from history is manifest in many of the behavior patterns of a great number of those people who are taking part in the new revolution of consciousness: the continuing movement of youth away from the institutional churches and synagogues; the widespread revival of interest in magic, astrology, and the occult; the use of drugs; and the turn to Eastern religions. Eastern mysticism in a sense denies the reality of time, and in so doing it reduces the importance of history in human affairs. It asserts that eternity or *nirvana* is to be found in the here-and-now of the present moment. The Eastern mystic therefore ridicules the modern Western mentality that seeks to explain the meaning of existence through cause-and-effect relationships, living constantly in the past and in the future, using the past to predict and indeed to explain and manipulate the future.

Many of these sensitive persons who have had their foundations of spiritual life shaken by the shifting winds of historical relativism and who have experienced within themselves the terror of history, along with many representatives of the counter-culture, have found new meaning and an untapped resource of power in the revival and reappropriation of the concept of "myth." But the reversion to myth by members of the counter-culture has by-and-large been reactionary in character. Since myth and ritual are seized upon as an alternative to the attitudes and mores of the technocratic society which are grounded in modern science and technology, they are adopted precisely because they are irrational and not subject to empirical verification and technological control. The recovery of the category of myth within the counter-culture has been marked by an obvious anti-intellectualism and by a romantic tendency toward neo-primitivism and neo-tribalism. In short, the appeal to myth by members of the counter-culture is primarily a self-conscious attempt *to regress* into what Paul Ricoeur has called the immediacy of "primary naïveté," that is, into a pre-critical, undifferentiated state of unbroken, literal mythical consciousness. [7]

The exploration of myth throughout the remaining sections of my essay pursues another path than that taken by members of the counter-culture. I have been trained in the presuppositions and methods of modern literary-historical criticism and have been shaken to the foundations by the vertigo and existential despair resulting from the awareness and experience of historical relativism. I am seeking to fill a spiritual vacuum by searching for a renewed sense of the meaning and power of myth — a sympathetic understanding of myth which is not antagonistic toward nor defensive against the critical methods and achievements of historical scholarship and the other social sciences. I share enthusiastically the new appreciation of the nature and function of myth resulting from more than a century of critical scholarship in a variety of fields — philosophy, theology, art history, literary criticism, philology, psychology, anthropology, sociology, and so on. The theory of myth expounded in my paper is characterized by a self-conscious effort *to progress* through the rational criticism of scientific and historical consciousness to a mediate, "second naïveté" — that is, to a meta-critical, differentiated state of broken, symbolic mythical consciousness. [8] The full development of that form of religious consciousness which Ricoeur has referred to as "second naïveté" presupposes a profound, imaginative, sympathetic understanding of primary naïveté and an equally deep exposure to rational criticism. Since second naïveté emerges on the other side of a form of criticism which is no longer reductive but restorative (that is, a criticism which seeks to transcend itself by means of criticism), the immediacy of belief in primitive naïveté is irremediably lost. The thorough-going application of critical reflection inevitably leads to "demythologization" in the sense that a symbolic image is recognized as a symbolic image and a myth is recognized as a myth. But "demythologization" does not necessarily imply "demythicization"; [9] rational reflection leads to the further recognition that symbolic images and myths cannot be replaced by or translated into scientific and philosophical-ontological substitutes. A myth which is understood as a myth but not removed or replaced is what Paul Tillich has called a "broken myth," that is, it is "broken" in its immediacy or literalness; but the dissolution of the literal sense of a myth does not necessarily undermine its inherent, symbolic, evocative, revelatory power. [10]

The prevailing trait in the "modernity" of contemporary Western man is that of the rejection, forgetfulness, and repression of symbolic images into the unconscious levels of the psyche. These rejected, forgotten, and repressed symbolic images and myths must now paradoxically be relearned and restored to consciousness by means of the methods and achievements of those very scientific disciplines which to so large an extent were responsible for "breaking" them and leading to their demise in power. Moreover, in the very process of seeking an imaginative, sympathetic understanding of symbolic images and myths, one invites these symbols and myths to make their own direct and non-rational or unconscious impact on him through a "living intuition" of their "rightness," "inevitability," and "truth." For there is always the real possibility that a symbolic image or a myth may free itself from its repression and all of its profanizations and come to life again through the evocative, revelatory power inherent within it. The next two sections of this essay focus upon some of the symbolic images and myths by means of which man has expressed and communicated his experience of transcendent mystery precipitated by his encounter with the future.

II. THE MYSTERY OF THE FUTURE AND MYTH

Because of his historical consciousness, modern Western man thinks of himself as a finite, conditioned being who has a past, a present, and a future. The flow of time moves ineluctably from an as yet unrealized future through a momentary present which instantly passes into an irrecoverable past. The painful consciousness of this constant flow of time causes grave anxiety and desperate activity on the part of man. In the words of Blaise Pascal:

> We do not rest satisfied with the present. We anticipate the future as too slow in coming, as if in order to hasten its course; or we recall the past, to stop its too rapid flight. So imprudent are we that we wander in the times which are not ours, and do not think of the only one which belongs to us; and so idle are we that we dream of those times which are no more, and thoughtlessly overlook that which alone exists. For the present is generally painful to us. We conceal it from our sight, because it troubles us; and if it be delightful to us, we regret to see it pass away. We try to sustain it by the future, and think of arranging matters which are not in our power, for a time which we have no certainty of reaching.

> Let each one examine his thoughts, and he will find them all occupied with the past and the future. We scarcely ever think of the present; and if we think of it, it is only to take flight from it to arrange the future. The present is never our end. The past and the present are our means; the future alone is our end. So we never live, but we hope to live; and, as we are always preparing to be happy, it is inevitable we should never be so.[11]

Man's distress and dissatisfaction with his state of ignorance and consequent lack of rational control over what the unknown future will bring are reflected in the perennial concern for and the present revival of interest in various forms of occult divination: astrology, numerology, palm reading, fortune telling, tarot cards, the I-Ching, and so on. Predictably, the more turbulent the present historical era becomes, the more traditional customs and moral guidelines of a culture are obliterated; and the more uncertain the future becomes, the greater becomes man's anxiety and the consequent demand (and hope) for preliminary glimpses and predictions of future events.

Man may take either a positive or a negative attitude toward the future. Hope is the positive, as anxiety is the negative, mode of awaiting the future. Again, man may relate himself to the future in an attitude of passive or of active expectation. He may make plans and projects in order to shape the future according to his wishes. Such an active attitude often leads man to regard himself optimistically as the master of his own destiny. Rather than waiting for the future to come to him from without, the active man goes toward it, anticipating and controlling it. The life and thought of modern Western man has been dominantly characterized by this active attitude through which he seeks progressively to control his future. By expanding his technological control over both his natural and his social environments, man the rational planner and organizer seeks a constant increase of the means whereby his dependence and insecurity are progressively diminished and his power to determine the future correspondingly increased.

But nothing can altogether conceal from man the fact that he is very far from being the unqualified arbiter of his future. He cannot remain unaware that his power and freedom to shape the future are limited because they are dependent on factors over which he has no control. One such factor is nature; another is the behavior of his fellow human beings. But man's precarious existence is most severely burdened by his anxious anticipation of his own death. From experiencing the painful loss of others through death, he arrives at the certainty that he too must die sometime. In fact, the only thing that man knows for certain about the future is that he and all of his loved ones will die. Perhaps the most singular feature of man setting him off from the rest of the animal kingdom is the fact that his life is a conscious "being unto death." He alone lives in anxious anticipation of death, is aware of its coming. This sure knowledge of the imminence of death lies like a shadow over his whole life. He alone knows what he loses in death. But it is precisely this inescapable death which man least understands and finds least imaginable. Experience offers him no point of comparison; he will know what it means only when he undergoes it. Thus, the death of man is surrounded by mystery, surmise, anxious expectation, and uncertainty.

All attempts to give a sense of meaning, purpose, and destiny to life from within the context of earthly historical existence come to grief on the fact of death. Death is the most difficult obstacle to hope. The conviction that life is really a being unto death tends to render stale and empty everything that fills man's fleeting days. Knowledge that the creators and guardians of the values of society and culture are in the end mercilessly dismissed and plunged into an abyss of nothingness undermines the ultimate worth of those values. Knowledge that death is unavoidable can only temporarily be displaced by a restless pursuit of changing tasks and diversions. The certain knowledge that he will die is also accompanied by hope that he will not die. For it is just as inherent in man to hope beyond death as it is inherent in man to know about his own approaching death. Man's awareness of the future compels him to push the question about himself and his destiny forward beyond death. Hence, widely spread among all peoples at all times is the belief in life after death. From primitive animism to the philosophical doctrine of immortality is the idea of a survival of the soul after death; equally widespread have been the beliefs of reincarnation and the transmigration of souls, or beliefs in some kind of resurrection of the body.[12]

Man's openness to the future and his deep-seated disposition toward hope drive him again and again to take a chance on the future and to hope for an abundant happiness from it. The skeptical David Hume has caught the essence of this stubborn human tendency toward hope:

Ask yourself, ask any of your acquaintance, whether they would live over again the last ten or twenty years of their life. No: but the next twenty, they say, will be better. . . . Thus, at last, they find (such is the greatness of human misery, it reconciles even contradictions) that they complain at once of the shortness of life and of its vanity and sorrow.[13]

Man's emotional response to the uncertainty and unpredictability of the future provides one of the contexts in which may occur that unique religious experience which Rudolf Otto has described in terms of the *mysterium tremendum et fascinans*. For an encounter with the Holy may be precipitated through man's anxiety-laden anticipation of the future before which he recoils in terror and yet which irresistibly arouses his curiosity and fascination. Such experiences of transcendent mystery are a primary and irreducible — though by no means exclusive — element in all "true religion"; they are the most powerful factor in keeping religious affections and consciousness alive.

The principal constituent in such experiences of the numinous is a certain kind of feeling or mood (*Stimmung*). Since the sense of the numinous or transcendent mystery impinges upon human consciousness as a feeling or mood, it cannot be fully grasped within the categories of rational conceptualization. Therefore, words can only be used metaphorically and indirectly to depict the underlying feeling or mood through the poetic or imaginative intuition of symbolic images. Symbolic images are verbal utterances which are not direct descriptions of feeling but are rather descriptions of concrete external objects, scenes, or actions which express or evoke feelings by the indirect but powerful workings of association or suggestion. The symbolic images are the expressive forms of determinate feeling experiences, that is, the symbolic images are themselves the form in which the feeling experiences have been brought to conscious awareness. Since the symbolic images contain within themselves the reality which they express and evoke, they cannot be translated or reduced into language which is directly descriptive and functions only at the sign level of signification.

Although the feeling which is predominant in an experience of transcendent mystery is originally awe and dread, that feeling in its later and more refined forms resolves itself ultimately into "a feeling of wholeness." In an experience of transcendent mystery, the self is affected by a whole or a totality which transcends and at the same time encloses the person having the experience. The kind of whole or totality which is perceived in the experience of transcendent mystery is an all-encompassing, all-embracing whole. Since the self perceiving the whole has a position within the whole, the person cannot stand outside the whole to observe it clearly and describe it literally. The person can only "feel" his way into the whole, or feel himself to be a part of the whole, or feel the whole to be present within himself. Feeling thus perceives through participation; the feeling-perception of the whole is immediate and non-discursive because the one perceiving is a part of the whole which is perceived. The experience or feeling of wholeness becomes conscious and can only be expressed through symbolic images.

A myth incorporates such symbolic images in an imaginative, numinous story which relates a dramatic act or series of events of cosmic significance. The definition of a myth as "an imaginative story" means that it is a narrative which may or may not be based upon historical fact but which, nevertheless, has a structure of temporality, that is, it has a beginning, a middle, and an end. The designation of a myth as "a *numinous* story" means that the narrative has grown out of some experience of transcendent mystery, that is, out of some encounter with the Holy or of some feeling-perception of all-encompassing wholeness. By "an act or series of events of cosmic significance" is meant some paradigmatic act or series of events which is understood to be of decisive importance for the world, particularly the world of men. What may be called "a complete myth" is a complex unity of mythic stories which sets forth a drama of universal significance in which individual persons may participate, thereby giving meaning, purpose and structure to human life with all of its fluctuating pleasure and pain, joy and despair, happiness and misery. The transforming power of the complete myth can make physical pain, personal loss and sacrifice, the helpless contemplation of the agony of others, and even death itself not only tolerable but full of meaning and purpose. It is not suffering and death which are the problem so much as empty, meaningless suffering and death. Myth enables the anxious sufferer to feel that he is participating in a cosmic drama transcending his private existence and in which his personal pain and suffering and death are seen as a significant part of this larger meaningful whole. Then man's pain and death may still be terrible and heart-rending; but they are not finally unendurable.

III. MYTH AND THE MYSTERY OF THE FUTURE

Modern Western man's awareness of the relentless passage of time and of the irreversibility of history leaves him in desperate need for some kind of myth which contains symbolic images that unify time — past, present, and future — into an all-embracing, all-encompassing whole. Modern man shares with men of all times and of all religions a need for mythic time, a time that makes all things new and gives meaning and value to the otherwise absurd existence of individuals and societies.

Yet this need for myth comes at the very time when the religious myth and symbolism of Judaism and Christianity has either been radically secularized or discarded. This secularization or rejection of the mythic symbolism of Judaism and Christianity has been the consequence of the more general "breaking of myth" in modern times. The rise of modern scientific and historical consciousness has led to the hard-won differentiation of scientific knowledge, cosmic process, history, and philosophical metaphysics from "myth." The primary reason for the rejection of traditional Jewish and Christian myths was that myth came to be conceived of as "falsehood" or "unwarranted superstition"; or it was understood to be an outworn, prescientific, historically conditioned mode of thought which had little or nothing to do with the essence of religious faith; or it was thought to veil a subjective, spiritual truth in objective categories which must now be translated into different categories of thought which are more consistent with the modern world view.

There is, however, a more adequate and satisfactory way of dealing with "broken myths." Without burying their heads in the sand by suspending all critical faculties so that they can relapse into the undifferentiated thinking of two thousand years ago, many persons who consciously recognize myth as myth still acknowledge its validity and indispensability. Myth is here accepted as the only possible and proper linguistic expression of religious experiences of transcendent reality. Myth so recognized and retained must, nevertheless, be interpreted within the context of its own category-system and in terms of its own criteria of truth. Myth must also be expected and allowed to function in its own proper sociological and psychological dimensions — for example, to secure social identity and cohesion, or to assure the individual that he is participating in a cause greater than himself by creating the hopeful expectation of happiness and well-being hereafter.

The primary reason for seeking to reevaluate and reappropriate the inherent power which still resides within the symbolic imagery and myths of Judaism and Christianity is that these two religious traditions have been and remain the dominant religious influences on the thought and existence of modern Western man, including the emergence of his scientific and historical mode of consciousness.

The assertion that Judaism and Christianity represent the meaning and value of the temporal process in terms of mythical imagery is made in opposition to those theologians, philosophers of religion, and historians of religion who argue that the word "myth" should be reserved only for "natural myths." "Natural myths," according to this view, are grounded in the natural rhythms of the cosmos where space is predominant over time, time is understood to be cyclic and repetitive, and the divine is experienced as immanent in nature. Natural myths locate man in society and place society in the cyclical and therefore repeatable processes of nature. Archaic man is said to have a sense of meaning and purpose because he is part of a larger social whole, which in turn participates in an even larger cosmic whole. The distinctiveness of Judaism and Christianity, according to this view, is found in the overcoming or supercession of mythic thought because God is made transcendent to nature and the cosmos, time becomes predominant over space and becomes linear and purposive rather than cyclic, and historical events rather than nature become infused with ultimate meaning and significance. This sharp distinction between mythical religions and historical religions also lies behind such over-simplified dichotomies as "peasant, agrarian religion" (epiphany gods that sanctify land, life, and culture) and "nomadic religion of the wilderness or desert" (a God on the move who demands decision and trust from his chosen people as he leads them into a historical future which is the goal of things taking place in the present).

This interpretation of "myth" is far too narrow and restrictive; or, better, it is incomplete. A more accurate and adequate interpretation makes a distinction between "natural myth" (which is defined in the sense of "myth" as outlined in the paragraph above) and "historical myth." Judaism and Christianity are religions which make use of historical myth. Both religious traditions hold that certain actual, historical, events reveal to the eyes of the faithful the key or clue to the understanding of the whole of human existence and destiny. This clue is offered to individual believers as the framework by which they may "make sense" of the ultimate mysteries of the universe, including the essential problems of man's origin and final destiny.

For example, Judaism takes the prophetic interpretation of events clustering around the origins of Israel as a nation as a key or clue for making sense of such ultimate mysteries, for feeling oneself to be part of a meaningful, value-producing, all-embracing whole. The specific events focus upon the deliverance of the Hebrews from Egyptian bondage (the Exodus), the giving of the Law and the establishment at Mount Sinai of the covenant relationship of the people with God, and the gift of the promised land. This distinctive belief in the covenant relationship with God, derived from certain crucial historical experiences through which the Hebrews as a nation had passed, was eventually projected forward to account in a symbolic way for the consummation of history (the Messianic Age, the Kingdom of God). The idea of the temporal beginning of the world can be expressed and communicated only in terms of the symbolic images which are imaginatively intuited and then incorporated into myth, not in the logical-descriptive categories of scientific prose. For the idea of a time before time began or of the beginning of time is literally inconceivable, as is also the idea of an infinite time which had no beginning. Whereas the myth of creation affirms that the God of Israel is the Cause of all that exists ("In the beginning, God created the heaven and the earth"), so the other declares that the God of Israel is the End or Goal of history (the Messianic Age, the Rule of God). The complete Jewish myth, which presents the universal drama in which all men and peoples willingly or unwillingly play their respective roles, interprets the meaning and value of human existence and the historical process itself in terms of the symbolic imagery of creation, sin, and ultimate redemption and consummation.

Likewise, Christianity arises out of a prophetic-apostolic interpretation of certain events which become symbolic images accounting for the ultimate mysteries of the universe and of man's being and destiny. All the meaning that was compressed into Jesus' life, death, and resurrection was expanded backward to encompass past history, and forward to embrace future history and finally its consummation in his Second Coming. Jesus Christ becomes the instrument of the creation ("Without him was not made anything which was made"), and the origin is also present in the goal. But the goal of the world and of history is also Christ and his rule with the Father; the myth of the Second Coming depicts the goal of the world as the triumph of God and his Christ. Hence, Christianity also has myths about the beginning and the end of the world and, therefore, of the temporal process as a Whole. The complete myth depicts a dynamic process of movement, a cosmic drama of creation, fall, and redemption in which individuals are called to participate creatively and actively in cooperation with the divine plan.

The primary direction of biblical historical myth is clearly from the center of a series of historical events toward the past and the primordial creation of all things and also, just as importantly, toward the future and the consummation of history. However, this emphasis upon the dominance of historical myth should not obscure the active presence in both Judaism and Christianity of natural myth. For cyclical, repetitive time is intimately bound up with the rhythmical, seasonal changes of nature manifested in the major festivals of the Jewish and Christian liturgical years. Events of the distant past or anticipations of distant future events can become existentially significant and relevant in the present only insofar as they are lifted out of the specific temporal contexts of their occurrence and taken as symbolic images of continuing, universal situations. The Exodus of the Israelites from Egypt, for example, would be for the modern Jew no more than an antiquarian datum, were it not transfigured in myth into a symbolic image of his people's continuous experience, an evidence of God's continuous design and providence, and an exemplification of all men's continuous progress out of their Egypts, forward to their Sinais, and thence, through trial in the wilderness, to the entry of their children into the inheritance of the promised land. Likewise, the Christian yearns to return repeatedly to the time of Jesus' birth, crucifixion, and resurrection as the time of a new beginning, a new creation, a cosmic renewal; and in the seasonal ritual of the liturgical year believers cyclically relive and reenact the life of the creator and redeemer of time. Christ is not just the one who has once and for all redeemed the present by his action in the past; nor is he simply the one who at some future point will come again. He is the one who comes again and again, bearing the redeemed past, illumining and sanctifying the present, and leading into the future toward a certain and glorious end. Natural myth with its cyclical model of time, and historical myth with its model of linear time, are not necessarily contradictory or mutually exclusive; both are present in Judaism and Christianity, although the cyclical model is decisively subordinated to the linear model.

Furthermore, if one accepts the distinction between "natural myth" and "historical myth," it becomes clear that if history has ultimate meaning, this meaning is not historical in the narrow sense of the term, but is rather mythical.[14] When one speaks of "the meaning of history," taken as an all-inclusive whole (that is, in its entirety and universality), he is actually speaking about the ultimate meaning and destiny of human existence, and this is not a question for the historian as historian. For in this case what is being spoken about is not that which has happened (and this is the only field in which historians are competent), but rather that which is to happen, and is to happen precisely because it "must happen." Neither "the ultimate" nor "the future" belongs to the realm of the empirical discipline of history, which is, by definition, limited to the understanding of the human past, and at most, the present in the light of the past. Historical predictions, of necessity, are conjectural and precarious extrapolations. Histories of men and societies are history, but the history of man, a truly universal and providential history, is no longer just history.[15]

Hence, much of what has been called "philosophy of history" or "universal history" is really "theology of history," which in turn is dependent upon historical myth.[16] For example, the recent movement in Christian theology associated with Jürgen Moltmann and Wolfhart Pannenberg, is based upon historical myth (or eschatology). This theological movement seizes upon the resurrection of Jesus as the key to the final meaning of history. The end or goal of universal history is understood to be present "proleptically" in the resurrection of Jesus of Nazareth. In Jesus' particular resurrection from the dead, the general resurrection of all men as the final end of universal history has been anticipated. Only knowledge of the end or goal of history, it is argued, can provide the perspective necessary for making sense of the total course of history. In this theology, the anticipated coming of the end of history in the midst of history actually forms the basis from which history as a mythic whole becomes comprehensible as a cosmic drama in which one can meaningfully participate.

Moltmann's theology of hope has correctly, I believe, discerned that the Christian's participation in Christ's resurrection, the hope of his own resurrection, is obscured in this present life by the experience of the cross. For, so far as man's present life is concerned, it must be concluded that there are both good and evil, happiness and sorrow, redeemed and unredeemed sinners. Any revision of this verdict must depend upon lengthening out the temporal perspective until it reaches a new and better conclusion. If there is to be any eventual resolution of the dialectical interplay between good and evil, and any decisive bringing of good out of evil, it must lie beyond the present moment and beyond the enigma of death. The belief in life beyond the grave is based upon the hope that beyond death God will resurrect or re-create or reconstitute human existence in both its inner and its outer aspects.

The Christian hope in the future completion and transformation of the temporal process is depicted in the symbolic imagery of the Kingdom of God. The golden age is projected on the historical screen of the future. The Christian claim is that the ultimate life of man lies in that Kingdom of God which is portrayed in the teaching of Jesus as a state of exultant and blissful happiness, symbolized as a joyous Messianic banquet in which all who have accepted God's gracious invitation rejoice together. Christian hope points forward to that final blessedness which will render meaningful and worthwhile all the pain, suffering, sacrifice, and wickedness that have occurred on the way to it. The past and present sufferings of men will in the end lead to the enjoyment of a common good which will be unending and therefore unlimited, and which will be seen by its participants as justifying any finite suffering endured in the course of attaining it. Christian hope, therefore, is not content simply to look toward the past to find the origins of suffering and death, but looks toward the future, expecting a triumphant resolution in the eventual perfect fulfillment of God's good purpose. The only way the nature of this anticipated ultimate fulfillment can be grasped by the finite mind of the Christian man of faith is indirectly and figuratively through the imaginatively intuited, symbolic images incorporated in Christian myth.

NOTES

[1] These two general assumptions are equally fundamental and potent presuppositions of the modern age. Note well, also, that "science" and "history" are *not* referred to as "the myths" or as constituent parts of "the essential myth" of modern man. Although science and history *function* in many striking ways in modern society as myth *functions* in primitive or archaic societies, I believe that such a broad and extended use of the term "myth" leads to an unwarranted ambiguity and confusion of meaning in the technical use of language. Therefore, throughout my essay, I try to distinguish "myth" as clearly and consistently as possible from "metaphysics," "ontology," and "science." "Metaphysics" or "ontology" is a self-conscious, carefully reasoned philosophical theory about the nature of being or what is ultimately real; it selects a key-idea or category drawn from some particular science or from some definite field of experience and analogically employs it to interpret or "make sense of" the whole universe, the whole of human experience, reality, or "the scheme of things entire." For further discussion of the relationship between myth, metaphysics or ontology, and science, see footnote 6 below.

[2] The seventeenth and early eighteenth centuries did not develop an "empirical" conception of history because of the authority of the classical Greek legacy. The Greeks had no conception of development in history; for them history was cyclical, and their golden age was in the past. Although modified in the Christian era by its having been uneasily united with the biblical view of history as linear, and as having a beginning and an ending, the classical view of history generally dominated the mind of the seventeenth and eighteenth century and prevented the emergence of any conception of a real development in history or of real changes in man's condition. Thus, even though the roots of modern historical consciousness may certainly be traced back to Hebrew and Christian interpretations of events as providential and time as linear rather than cyclical, the Hebrew and Christian perspective has been secularized and naturalized in the modern era. The secular vision of evolution and progress have replaced an earlier faith in divine providence and an eschatological outlook toward a future fulfillment. We must be careful not to transpose our modern and secular historical thinking into the "historical consciousness" of the Old and New Testaments. See Karl Löwith, *Meaning in History* (Chicago: The University of Chicago Press, 1949), pp. 19, 186.

[3] Carl Becker, *The Heavenly City of the Eighteenth-century Philosophers* (New Haven: Yale University Press, 1932), p. 19.

[4] The understanding of nature as history is explained as follows by R. G. Collingwood: "Modern cosmology, like its predecessors, is based on an analogy. What is new about it is that the analogy is a new one. . . . The modern view of nature, which first begins to find expression towards the end of the eighteenth century and ever since then has been gathering weight and establishing itself more securely down to the present day, is based on the analogy between the processes of the natural world as studied by natural scientists and the vicissitudes of human affairs as studied by historians. . . . Modern cosmology could only have arisen from a widespread familiarity with historical studies, and in particular with historical studies of the kind which placed the conception of process, change, development in the centre of their picture and recognized it as the fundamental category of historical thought. This kind of history appeared for the first time about the middle of the eighteenth century." *The Idea of Nature* (New York: Oxford University Press, 1960), pp. 9-10; see also pp. 174-77.

[5]See Mircea Eliade, *Cosmos and History; The Myth of the Eternal Return* (New York: Harper & Brothers, 1959), ch. 4.

[6]Alvin Toffler has perceptively described this loss or destruction of human freedom in his analysis of the new psychological disease which he calls "future shock." Future shock is the dizzying disorientation brought on by the technologically caused premature arrival of the future. In his discussion of the dangers of "overchoice," Toffler points out that there comes "a time when choice, rather than freeing the individual, becomes so complex, difficult, and costly, that it turns into its opposite. There comes a time, in short, when choice turns into overchoice and freedom into un-freedom." *Future Shock* (New York: Bantam Books, Inc., 1971), p. 283.

[7]Paul Ricoeur, *The Symbolism of Evil* (New York: Harper & Row, 1967), esp. pp. 347-57.

[8]The most prevalent historical-evolutionary theory of myth has been and probably remains that human consciousness has evolved from religious myth through rational metaphysics to empirical science. This paper presupposes an alternative historical-evolutionary theory of man's intellectual development which preserves the values of modern science and its technology without the rejection of metaphysics or ontology as a legitimate philosophical enterprise, and without the rejection of all intuitive knowledge embodied by aesthetic symbolic images, myths, and rituals. This alternate theory affirms that man's intellectual development has moved from an undifferentiated to a differentiated kind of thinking. According to this view, "primitive" or "archaic" thinking, while predominantly mythical, is not wholly mythical. On the contrary, myths, speculative hypotheses, and empirical descriptions all interpenetrate each other in an undifferentiated way. They are all equally "primordial." No mode of primitive understanding is superseded or eliminated during the development of human understanding. They all persist, although one or another will tend to be dominant at one time or another. Man first learns to identify them, then orders them, and finally in the modern period separates them into independent realms. This process of intellectual differentiation has made mythical knowledge, metaphysical knowledge, and scientific knowledge increasingly powerful in the modern world. For a fuller exposition of this "differentiation theory" of myth, see Herbert W. Richardson, *Toward an American Theology* (New York: Harper & Row, 1967), pp. 50-51. The essence of this theory of intellectual differentiation can also be found in Philip E. Slater, *Microcosm: Structural, Psychological and Religious Evolution in Groups* (New York: John Wiley & Sons, Inc., 1966), pp. 144-45.

[9]Paul Ricoeur has argued for a distinction between "demythologization" and "demythicizing." According to Ricoeur, modern man now lives in an age where history and myth have become separate or dissociated. Myth is now consciously and critically recognized as myth. Mythical time can no longer be coordinated with the time of events that are "historical" in the sense required by historical method and historical criticism; mythical space can no longer be coordinated with modern knowledge of geography. This critical awareness hastens the movement of demythologization, which is the removal of the pseudo-knowledge or false logos of myth. Demythologization is the counterpart of an ever more rigorous decision about what is history according to modern historical method. Yet demythologization, that is, the dissolution of myth as literal-historical explanation, is for Ricoeur the necessary way to the restoration of myth as symbol. See *The Symbolism of Evil*, esp. pp. 161-62, 349-50.

[10]Paul Tillich, *Dynamics of Faith* (New York: Harper & Row, 1957), esp. pp. 48-54.

[11]Blaise Pascal, *Pensées*, ed. and trans. W. F. Trotter (New York: Everyman, 1943), no. 172, pp. 49-50.

[12]Historical knowledge and relativism forces recognition of the fact that man's awareness of the future leads to culturally different notions about the nature and value of an afterlife. For example, many Eastern men regard the afterlife as a curse or condemnation rather than a desirable reward. Yet even here, this notion of the afterlife is ultimately attained by the "wise" or "enlightened ones"; most Eastern men remain bound to the realm of illusion (*maya*) and the wheel of fluctuating birth-death-and-rebirth (*samsara*) because they remain emotionally attached to life in this world and hope for continued existence after death.

[13]David Hume, *Dialogues Concerning Natural Religion*, ed. Henry D. Aiken (New York: Hafner, 1957), pp. 65-66.

[14]I agree with Karl Löwith when he says: "To the critical mind, neither a providential design nor a natural law of progressive development is discernible in the tragic human comedy of all times." *Meaning in History*, p. v. Therefore, the words of Reinhold Niebuhr remain an accurate analysis of the historian's situation: "It is impossible to interpret history at all without a principle of interpretation which history as such does not yield. The various principles of interpretation current in modern culture, such as the idea of progress or the Marxist concept of an historical dialectic, are all principles of interpretation introduced by faith. They claim to be conclusions about the nature of history at which men arrive after a 'scientific' analysis of the course of events; but there can be no such analysis of the course of events which does not make use of some presupposition of faith as the principle of analysis or interpretation." *The Nature and Destiny of Man*, 1 (New York: Charles Scribner's Sons, 1941): 151.

[15]R. G. Collingwood has underscored the fact that, since the historian has no special gift of prophecy or divination, he can deal only with the human past and present, while the future is and must remain a closed book to him: "This reference to a future age betrays an important characteristic of medieval historiography. If challenged to explain how he knew that there was in history any objective plan at all, the medieval historian would have replied that he knew it by revelation; it was part of what Christ had revealed to man concerning God. And this revelation not only gave the key to what God had done in the past, it showed us what God was going to do in the future. The Christian revelation thus gave us a view of the entire history of the world, from its creation in the past to its end in the future, as seen in the timeless and eternal vision of God. Thus medieval historiography looked forward to the end of history as something foreordained by God and through revelation foreknown to man; it thus contained in itself an eschatology. Eschatology is always an intrusive element in history. The historian's business is to know the past, not to know the future; and whenever historians claim to be able to determine the future in advance of its happening, we may know with certainty that something has gone wrong with their fundamental conception of history." *The Idea of History* (New York: Oxford University Press, 1956), p. 54; see also pp. 120, 220.

[16]The term "philosophy of history" is here used in the speculative sense of a systematic rational interpretation of universal history in accordance with a (non-historical) principle by which historical events and successions are unified and directed toward an ultimate meaning. "Philosophy of history" in this speculative sense is to be distinguished from contemporary *critical* philosophy of history, that is, philosophical criticism of the kind of thinking which we call historical, the methods used by historians, the nature of historical "facts," and so on. A "theology of history" openly confesses that its interpretation of history is based upon revelation rather than upon philosophical reasoning. Taken in the speculative sense, philosophy of history is dependent on theology of history, in particular on the theological or mythical concept of history as a history of fulfillment and salvation. Therefore, neither speculative philosophy of history nor theology of history are "scientific" in the sense of accepting and working within the limits of empirical methods.

Myth and History
as Complementary Modes of
Consciousness

CORNELIA DIMMITT CHURCH

MUST we choose between myth and history? In the search for knowledge, certainty, truth or the bases of religious faith are these real alternatives? Two extremes present themselves today, neither of which is entirely satisfying by itself as a way of providing criteria for certainty. One, the mythic attitude, suggests we know because we project predisposed archetypal configurations, mental patterns, onto external circumstances. In this view knowledge is a re-cognition and truth subjective, a matter of personal perspective. The other extreme is that of scientific history[1] where meaning or truth is revealed through the amassing of externally derived facts. What is the truth of a situation is objectively deduced from historical events.

Although there are other less radically opposed ways in which the terms myth and history are understood today, and the opposition pictured above is extreme, why is it that these alternatives seem so often to present themselves as mutually exclusive options? In popular as well as scholarly contexts, myth is repeatedly dismissed by definition as falsehood while history is accepted as truth. Myth and reality are opposed in daily headlines and in the titles of books; the quest for the historical Jesus seems for some to be a search to prove the truth of biblical faith through its basis in historical fact. There appears to be a conflict between two ways of viewing reality that have become constellated around these two terms and pursuits which are then viewed as polar opposites. Are these really two mutually exclusive modes of perception requiring the adoption of one to the exclusion of the other? Or is there not a congenial way to accept the complementarity of these functions in human life? I believe there is, if myth and history can be understood to be complementary modes of consciousness which may work congruently to perceive and express the same symbolic view of the world. It is, as I will suggest in what follows, in their very coincidence that the experience of certainty lies. When known reality, the domain of history, and archetypal image, the realm of myth, coincide, only then can knowledge, certainty, truth and/or faith be said to occur.

> Wherever known reality stops, where we touch the unknown, there we project an archetypal image.[2]

Even to speak of "the unknown" is to admit that there are other dimensions to existence than those directly accessible to consciousness. In the religious language of Western traditions the term "transcendent" has been used to describe that which man does not perceive with his senses as external reality but which he

35

nevertheless perceives to exist. Psychologists have called this simply "unconscious." In using these terms, man seems to recognize some relationship between what he calls known and unknown, or conscious and unconscious, or himself and God, and this relationship is maintained through symbolic activity. A symbol is a means of expressing something rationally inexpressible in terms of something concrete, for example, a wooden cross. Religious language is always symbolic for it speaks of the transcendent, or of transcendent qualities that cannot be expressed otherwise. Although common words are used, they are used in a sense other than the empirical. A cross is empirically two joined sticks of wood. Symbolically in the Christian tradition the cross represents the suffering, death, resurrection, and saving powers of Jesus as God in ways not adequately explained by a descriptive sentence like this one. Louis Dupré says in *The Other Dimension*:

> The symbolic must be based upon the non-symbolic to become intelligible . . . [But] the whole dictionary of religion consists of metaphors . . . The ability of symbols to express a transcendent reality is the ultimate reason why religious man cannot dispense with them.[3]

The language of religion is symbolic; its phrases are metaphors giving meaning and structure to existence. The question asked of any religious tradition should not be whether or not its claims are "true," but what are its basic metaphors. Religious belief is understood within its own tradition as Absolute Truth, but from outside as metaphor. Does the source of such metaphors lie in external events, historical facts, or in inner dispositions, possibly archetypes? Does the metaphor precede the perception of an event or is the event the occasion for symbolic interpretation? Was Jesus indeed God who appeared in history or is the idea of Christ a symbolic view of the man called Jesus? To return to von Franz's quote, in finding meaning in historical events do we project our own "archetypal" patterns onto them or do events themselves contain a certain meaning which they communicate to us? Is truth known chiefly by mythic or historical means?

Let us suppose that both processes occur at once. There is no meaning in events by themselves; there is no meaning apart from events. The historical event provokes an interpretation whose symbolic value results from a perceived analogy between inner and outer dimensions of a man's world: inner pattern and outer event coincide. This sort of coincidence between inner and outer describes the symbolic nature of thought. It is the centrality of certain symbols to a man's life that renders them what we call "religious." It is not easily possible to separate Jesus, the historical man, from Christ, the symbol. These two views of Jesus represent two components of the Christian's thinking processes, the historic and the mythic; one is primarily concerned with external event, the other more occupied with the interpretive functioning of the mind. Both together seek to relate the known and the unknown. Man's understanding is the union of historical event and archetypal pattern; knowledge and experience are the fruit of this union and symbolic activity the expression of it.

The current "crisis of historical consciousness" whose roots have been briefly summarized in the Introduction to this volume and need not be recapitulated here[4] is in large part due to a failure to recognize that biblical faith is now and has always been based on a particular symbolic view of the world that was forged out of certain historical events (exodus, Davidic kingdom, Jesus' ministry and crucifixion, etc.), but has never been grasped exclusively in terms of the purely historical nature of these events. As Kierkegaard points out, facts have never been sufficient to faith.[5] Events in themselves have no meaning. These historical events have been interpreted symbolically from their inception because they were originally viewed as the doings of God. And what cannot be fully known empirically, i.e., God and his purposes, can only be expressed in symbol.

The problem of our seminar, which I understand to be a conflict between mythic and historical views of biblical truth, strikes me as a soluble one for these views represent two human ways of thinking which are complementary and need not be opposed. It remains to show how they represent alternate modes of consciousness, how they have cooperated in the original biblical traditions, and how they may cooperate today in the appropriation of these traditions for faith. This paper will therefore have two principle parts, the first on myth and history as complementary modes of consciousness and the second on two critical biblical themes: *creation* in the Old Testament and *resurrection* in the New Testament. I will try to show how different modes of expression, hence consciousness, are found in the textual passages in which these themes are found. I will suggest that a common metaphor in each case is being bodied forth in different modes of expression, and I will conclude that the right question to ask of the Bible, of the tradition, and of one's personal faith, is not whether myth or history is the mode of truth, but what are the basic symbols or metaphors of the tradition that are found in both these modes, and beyond which one cannot go in the search for the roots of faith.[6]

II

Using the terms in a general sense, it may be fruitful to view myth and history as indicative of alternative and complementary modes of consciousness in man. R. Ornstein in *The Psychology of Consciousness* has surveyed recent discoveries in brain research in connection with age-old distinctions between these human functions to show they can be related to a structural dichotomy in the brain:

> The cerebral cortex of the brain is divided into two hemispheres, joined by a large bundle of interconnecting fibers called the "corpus callosum" . . . Both the structure and function of these two "half-brains" in some part underlie the two modes of consciousness which simultaneously coexist within each one of us. Although each hemisphere shares the potential for many functions, and both sides participate in most activities, in the normal person the two hemispheres tend to specialize. The left hemisphere (connected to the right side of the body) is predominantly involved with analytical, logical thinking, especially in verbal and mathematical functions. Its mode of operation is primarily linear. This hemisphere seems to process information sequentially [thinks historically] . . .
> If the left hemisphere is specialized for analysis, the right hemisphere (. . . connected to the left side of the body) seems specialized for holistic mentation. Its language ability is quite limited. This hemisphere is primarily responsible for our orientation in space, artistic endeavor, crafts, body image, recognition of faces. It processes information more diffusely than does the left hemisphere and its responsibilities demand a ready integration of many inputs at once. If the left hemisphere can be termed predominantly analytic and sequential in its operation,

then the right hemisphere is more holistic and relational, and more simultaneous in its mode of operation . . .[7]

The recognition that we possess two cerebral hemispheres which are specialized to operate in different modes may allow us to understand much about the fundamental duality of our consciousness. This duality has been reflected in classical as well as modern literature as between reason and passion, between mind and intuition. Perhaps the most famous of these dichotomies in psychology is that proposed by Sigmund Freud, of the split between the "conscious" mind and the "unconscious." The workings of the "conscious" mind are held to be accessible to language and to rational discourse and alteration; the "unconscious" is much less accessible to reason or to verbal analysis.[8]

Ornstein goes on to say that "the idea of the complementarity of two major modes of consciousness is hardly new . . . What is new is a recognition that these modes operate physiologically as well as mentally and culturally."[9] I would add that accepting the physiological bases of the complementarity of these modes may help us to accept their existence as equally valid aspects of being human between which we cannot choose. Furthermore, an interesting light is cast by this research on certain aspects of the mind identified by C. G. Jung wherein Conscious and Unconscious form the major components of the psyche, with Ego the regulative and directive mechanism and the Self a mediating factor. For there is a certain lack of communication between the two modes identified by Ornstein; the analytic mode is verbal, the holistic mode primarily non-verbal. To the verbal side, the non-verbal side is not accessible through consciousness. Experiments with people whose *corpus callosum* connecting the two hemispheres has been cut demonstrate this mutual inaccessibility.[10] So we may have here a particular way of looking at Jung's classifications: what is conscious consists of the verbal and analytic functions; what is not accessible to consciousness, or is unconscious, are the holistic functions. Through the activity of the Ego, these two groups of functions are balanced and integrated. The goal of realizing the Self (what Jung calls Individuation) may be understood as the finding of a single set of symbols in which both major psychic modes identified by Ornstein find resonant expression. Symbolic activity may be viewed as the expressing of a correspondence between the external world and the unconscious via the cooperative activity of the two hemispheres whose different functions correspond to the radical distinctions between external and internal reality. The left-brain functions relate more closely to outer events, the right-brain functions to archetypal experience; thus the hemispheres of the brain function as mediating modes of awareness and expression intermediate between the wholly external world and the wholly internal, the unconscious. Symbolism, then, is what we call the particular means through which these otherwise mutually inaccessible modes do in fact communicate. As the two sets of functions are largely inaccessible to each other by the means characteristic to each alone, it is only through the cooperation between them that symbolic activity occurs. And such symbolic activity is a necessary, natural human activity. Note in this context Stevenson's remark: "The essential character and direction of our personal and social lives are shaped by myth . . . It is the symbols within the context of the myth which give rise to all thought (cf. Ricoeur)."[11]

Myth and history, then, may both be described as symbolic modes of perception and expression that are continuous with each other but which emphasize different sorts of psychic activity: myth, the holistic, synthetic aspect in close touch with unconscious archetypal configurations; and history, the linear, analytic mode which is primarily verbal, in close touch with the reality of external events.

> Myths are verbally developed symbols.[12]
> History is just one damn thing after another.[13]

These quotations appear to reflect the same extreme attitudes outlined in the beginning of this paper, but it seems more appropriate to see the two as continuous, not opposed. If myth can be understood as verbally developed *symbol,* history can be seen as *verbally developed* symbol. To the degree that a symbol is verbally developed into narrative and story rather than simply image, and to the degree that the narrative depends upon external event, it becomes history. To the degree that history is depicted as representing exemplary situations, eternally true patterns, it is mythic. So both myth and history can be understood to be symbolic modes of perception and expression whose emphases and methods differ, but which function similarly to give meaning to existence.

Von Franz describes the continuous nature of these functions in terms of mind and world:

> What we call psyche and what we call matter are really only two aspects of one living phenomenon which if observed in an extraverted way and with extraverted methods from outside give results which physicists [and historians] describe, whereas if we describe it subjectively, from the inside we get . . .[14] [something like this, that creation myths reveal] not the origin of our cosmos but the origin of man's conscious awareness of the world.[15]

World and psyche, outer and inner, right-brain and left-brain are two poles of a continuum. Myth and history articulate these two potentially cooperative functions which are manifest in every man's life. And, I would say, it is when the two effectively reinforce each other, when a single symbol or metaphor is perceived in both modes together, as I hope to show is the case in the Bible, that knowledge, certainty, truth, and faith occur.

How does this work in a man's individual life? One's own personal history develops in a dialectical way, relating the unconscious, non-verbal dispositions of the psyche to external, historical events in one's life. As Stevenson says, "[without its ground in symbol and myth] historical experience would not be possible . . . Myth permeates our historical sense."[16] It is through our earliest childhood experiences that external events first evoke our archetypal predispositions, the unconscious patterns accessible to the holistic, right-brain side, which, as it were, fixate those events. Here our attitudes to life are formed, a union of inner predispositions with unique, specific, external events. And in this union, through it, in our earliest years, meanings are given foundation and a particular script for the rest of life is formed.[17]

How does this relate to myth and history in the Jewish and Christian traditions? In religious traditions, too, certain combinations of historical events and symbolic patterns lie at the beginning forming a script that continues to develop throughout the ongoing tradition, in which certain basic symbols, metaphors, patterns of thought remain constant but take new forms of expression in each subsequent age. As human experience and consciousness result from a union of holistic and analytic consciousness, of inner and outer events, through symbolic activity, so can the events and meanings of biblical tradition be understood not as myth *or* history, but as both myth *and* history, functioning cooperatively.

Louis Dupré uses a convenient term to describe the Hebraic perspective, *mythistory*, explaining it this way: "the transcendent, historical perspective of Israel did not exclude the mythical consciousness . . . The wedge of sacred history holds apart the golden age of the future from that of the past [both of which are mythical]."[18] History to the Israelites could be described as the absence of God, as that which happens to man cut off from God, in the intervals between his coming to save. In addition, the two, the divine and the natural, also interpenetrate because God acts through historical events. In the New Testament this same interpenetration of historical event and transcendent dimension, of history and myth, is clearly focused in the person of Jesus Christ who combines both in his own person. He is both God and man, both mythic and historic at one and the same time. Our questions of both Old and New Testaments seem to be: is it the historical experiences that preceded and determined the symbolic meaning (Yahweh has saved via exodus; Jesus has saved via his crucifixion)? Or was it a particular symbolic predisposition that permitted certain historical events to be understood as saving events? The answer must be both at once, the interpenetration of inner and outer, holistic and analytic, mythical and historical aspects. Dupré puts the question of biblical traditions this way: how can the purely historical ever attain a transhistorical status? How can a historical event (exodus, Jesus' life) convey a meaning and power to later generations? Only by the symbolic interpretation of that event. "Events become religious, and *a fortiori*, revelatory only in and through interpretation . . . [which indeed] may be done during its very occurrence."[19] Thus even in the very happening, event and meaning, history and myth coincide.

If we examine two critical biblical themes: *creation* in the Old Testament and *resurrection* in the New Testament, we will find each theme expressed in both modes, mythic and historical, in ways which make it impossible to separate the two. Asking "Which came first?" may prove to be a wholly inappropriate question to ask, deriving as it does from our predominately historical mode of thinking; therefore let us rather examine how the two modes cooperatively render the same symbolic view, in each case, and posit that it is in the symbolic congruence of these two modes that biblical faith lies.

III

The entire Old Testament celebrates creation, the creation of the people Israel as God's chosen people, chosen for a special relationship with him. In her view, Israel was to receive the special guardianship of God in return for her loving obedience in response. Thus creation, salvation, and convenant are three closely allied themes in the Old Testament, three basic symbolic statements you could say. God's salvation of Israel in the exodus and the wilderness were her creation; this relationship was sealed by the covenant at Sinai and made concrete in the conquest of Canaan where God's people finally gained land to live on and political existence as a nation among nations, where they in fact developed their self-awareness as Yahweh's people. The creation of the world and the creation of the nation of Israel are seen in the Old Testament as two analogous events having the same meaning: both natural world and the people Israel have their origin in God. The mythic views of world-creation and the historical event of the creation of the state of Israel represent two terms of a perceived analogy, neither of which can be clearly identified as prior. Mythic and historic creation are for the Israelites in the Old Testament two consequences of a single reality, God's creative power. From outside the tradition, we may put a question: Was it God's creation of the world that preceded God's creation of Israel? Or was it the consciousness of having been constituted a people after the conquest of Canaan that preceded the Israelites' awareness or claim that God created the world? Which gave rise to the other? Neither can be said to be wholly precedent,[20] the two awarenesses arose out of each other, a union of mythic and historic views expressed in the symbolic statement: God creates.

The subject of creation motifs in the Old Testament is a vast one. Let us look at four instances to see how in fact creation appears in both mythic and historic modes in different passages, and conclude by showing how in Ps 74 (cf. Ps 132, Job 38—41) these several modes have been quite naturally homologized within a single passage of the text itself.

Gen 1—2:4a. The creation of the physical world, including space and time, is depicted by Priestly writers (probably writing in exile in Babylon, ca. 6th or 5th c. BCE) as a means of showing God's power in creating the cosmic materiality. This natural creation is viewed as a first step in the creation of Israel as a nation; it is a means of showing the subordination of the astral deities of Mesopotamia to Israel's God, and probably was written also to legitimize the Sabbath and the whole idea of cult-festival times as necessary to the faith by referring their establishment to the seventh day of a temporally organized scheme of world creation. What is created? The physical world of nature: earth, waters, plants, animals, and mankind, and the non-terrestrial world of the universe which includes time: sun, moon, stars, and the alternation of night and day. In fact, an intimate connection between myth and history is evident in this first chapter of Genesis from the (mythical) formless void in which the Spirit of God moved before anything as it is now existed comes forth both spatial and temporal (historical) reality, the world as we know it now to be. From unknowable origins, spoken of only in mythic language ("the Spirit of God was moving over the face of the waters," v. 2) comes the beginning of historical time via the alternation of night and day, the establishment of the pattern of the week.

How then is this creation to be understood? It can be grasped as a central metaphor, a basic symbolic statement of the tradition, that has two prominent parts. The first, that man's empirical world both spatial and temporal derives from a transcendent reality which is named God, which is neither described nor understood fully, but which has creative power. And second, that this creation means the establishment of order, the determining of limits, the giving of form to the unformed. For example, note how God (v. 1-5) sets divisions to the reigning darkness, rendering it into alternating light and dark. Note how God separates in a similar fashion the pre-existent waters (v. 6, 7) from space ("the firmament"). Then how dry land is congealed from the midst of the waters (v. 9). And later how the lights of the firmament are made to light day and night in successive, orderly fashion (v. 14-16). In each case divisions are made, an orderly pattern of spatio-temporal reality is being established that echoes the orderly rule of man over nature (v. 26) and the rule of law in society that results from Moses' experience at Sinai (cf. Leviticus, etc.). Note certain key words that reveal this sense of order: "separated" (v. 4, 7, 14); "gathered together" (v. 10); "to rule" (v. 16, 18); and finally, in regard to the creation of mankind, "let them have dominion over the animals" (v. 26). What is the result of this disciplined order? Fruitfulness and prosperity: "plants yielding seed, fruit trees bearing fruit" (v. 12); to the fish: "be fruitful and multiply and fill the waters in the seas and let birds multiply on the earth (v. 22); and to man: "be fruitful and multiply and fill the earth and subdue it" (v. 28). The last quote epitomizes the burden of the metaphor for creation in Gen 1—2:4a: the interrelationship between fruitfulness and order, how *creation by the establishing of order* in this model leads to the prosperity of that which is created, through the ongoing provident activity of God, the source.[21]

Gen 2:4b—3:26. In this passage a different model of creation is presented, centering not on earth, sky, and time but on the creation of man and the nature of his relationship with God. It embodies most probably a desert, nomadic legend (from the J account, recorded ca. 10th or 9th c. BCE) and reflects a genuine concern for man's state as totally dependent on God. Man is formed by God as though by a potter from the dust of the ground combined with a watery mist, and given life by the influx of God's breath into his nostrils. And he is given by God a paradisiacal garden to live in and one commandment: not to eat of the tree of knowledge of good and evil.[22] He and his wife transgress this commandment and are consequently cast out of the perfection of paradise, he to work for his food, she to suffer in childbirth and be subject to the rule of her husband. Human existence as we know it begins as a result of this transgression. What is this myth saying metaphorically through this particular model of creation? Three meanings stand out: first, man is formed of earthly material, the dust; his nature is in part rooted in the material world. But secondly, man is dependent on God for his origin and existence. As dust he has no form until God molds him; formed, he has no life until God breathes his spirit into him (inspiration). As in Gen 1, the central metaphor is *creation by establishing order*, in this case the bodily shape of Adam is the first form order takes. Secondly, man's creation involves a covenantal relationship with his creator, an orderly, contractual relationship that demands obedience from man in return for providence from God. In Gen 1 man was created in God's image to rule and provide for other earthly creatures, hierarchically. In this account the relationship is explicitly contractual: God protects man only if he is obedient. Since Adam and Eve fail to be obedient, they are thrust out of Eden and thereby separated from God. We see again in this a paradigm for the relationship between myth and history. Eden represents the holistic domain of myth, continual close relationship with the transcendent which is what the whole idea of a perfect paradise conveys in mythic language. Leaving Eden represents the start of human history as we know it to be, full of ignorance, work, trials, suffering, and eventual death. History is therefore equivalent to estrangement from God in temporal terms, just like the invisibility of God is to the empirical world in spatial terms. As history is established in temporal terms in Gen 1, in Gen 2 and 3 it is established in moral, covenantal terms, through the personal relationship between man and God. History is God's absence effected by man's disobedience.

Finally, we see here the familiar metaphor of Gen 1, creation by establishing order, in different dress: first the giving of form to dust that is Adam's body and second by establishing a moral order that is equivalent to the conditions of the ongoing covenantal relationship: God protects his people in return for their loving obedience. The consequences of the failure of this order are made only too clear: man's misery in the absence of God, and the way the entire historical realm of existence in time becomes an example of the fruits of man's disobedience in Eden. Myth and history can be seen to be inseparable in this creation account; together in complementary fashion they express the central metaphor of creation by establishing order, including the peculiar possibility of the destruction of that order by man himself.[23]

Job 40, 41; Isa 51; Ps 74. Another collection of mythical creation motifs deals not only with God, the transcendent creator, but also with the apparent bestification of those forces opposing God in his creative acts, those strange, indescribable, demonic creatures Rahab, Behemoth, Leviathan, and the "dragons," the Taninim. All of these, like Tehom in Gen 1, appear to be relics of non-Hebraic myths (of undatable origin and used by later writers) who appear as the inchoate, terrifyingly powerful enemies of Yahweh threatening the destruction of his creation, the return of chaos or formlessness to overwhelm form. In the texts where they are mentioned God defeats and destroys them or reins them in, as it were, as part of his continuing creative activity. In the same way as the Spirit of God divides, limits, and gives order to Tehom in Gen 1, so does God control these creatures, mythic embodiments of the powers of disorder over order. Again, creation is viewed metaphorically as the establishing of order, in this case, in the effecting of control over the powers of chaos. And again in Job 40 and 41, God reciting his past creative acts to convey his nature to his questioner claims past victories over Behemoth and Leviathan as evidence of his powers. Note the means of his victories;

> Behold Behemoth, which I made as I made you;
>   he eats grass like an ox . . .
> Can one take him with hooks,
>   or pierce his nose with a snare? (40:14, 24)

In other words, can you do such as I have done? Note also:

> Can you draw out Leviathan with a fishhook,
>   or press down his tongue with a cord?
> Can you put a rope in his nose
>   or pierce his jaw with a hook? (41:1, 2)

Both enemies have been hooked, tamed, or controlled by snare and rope. the analogy between these mythical victories and the establishing of a convenantal relationship between God and Israel is clearly made in a closely following verse: "Will he make a covenant with you to take him for your servant forever?" (41:4)

Note in each case how the mythical beasts are hooked, snared, brought under Yahweh's control as a creative and salvational act, for by doing this the rest of the world is made safe for creation. In fact in Job, Isaiah, and certain Psalms (see below) these creatures are evoked in contexts wherein creation and salvation are clearly analogous events, just as the salvation of the tribes of Israel through exodus and wilderness events became equivalent to the creation of Israel as a political entity in the conquest: God did it all.[24] From God's standpoint creation is salvation; both are moments of the manifestation of the transcendent through historical reality. Hence both terms are symbolic, uniting transcendent and empirical, mythic and historic, God and man present to each other in the same place and time.

Deuteronomic History (Josh 1—12; Judg 1,2; Deut; 2 Sam; 1, 2 Kgs; Ps 132). Finally, let us look at the most evident historical accounts of creation in the Old Testament: the creation of Israel as a landed, political entity under King David. (The bulk of this material cited above is the work of the so-called Deuteronomic historians who appear to have edited accounts of the history of the establishment of the kingdom ca. 7th c. BCE.) As I indicated before, the Gen 1 account of the creation of the world was apparently written in exile after the establishment and subsequent demise of the Davidic kingdom. Mythical world-creation and historical state-creation are viewed under the same metaphor: God's bringing of order out of disorder, in the mythical case, the formless disorder of Tehom, and in the historical case, the unorganized, nomadic twelve tribes of Israel who first came together in the religious amphictyony at Shiloh after which the political kingdom of Israel under David came to be established. The actual history of these events can be found in the above cited passages. The establishment of the political kingdom had no necessary symbolic significance to those outside this tradition. That it was viewed by the Hebrews as the creative activity of God shows clearly their symbolic view of certain historical events. This was not the accomplishment of men, but the effect of the transcendent dimension of existence, God, working through the empirical. As God created man to rule in Gen 1, as man was formed out of dust in Gen 2, so is man in all ways dependent on God for his existence. The kingdom of David is then another salvific act of God like Exodus, Wilderness, Sinai, and Conquest, through which the creation of God's chosen people, Israel, is effected. Once again we see the alliance of mythic and historical views: political creation is equivalent to world creation from the standpoint of God.

Psalm 132 (v. 8-18) makes it quite clear that the rule of David was God's accomplishment and its continuation in the future depends on a continuation of the covenantal relationship between God and man throughout history, whose model we have already seen in the creation myth of Gen 2, 3:

> The Lord swore to David a sure oath
>   from which he will not turn back:
> "One of the sons of your body
>   I will set on your throne.
> If your sons keep my covenant
>   and my testimonies which I shall teach them,
> Their sons also forever
>   shall sit upon your throne" (Ps 132:11, 12).

To conclude, let us look finally at Ps 74 (cf. Job 38—41) which shows simply that both myth and history were congenial and complementary modes of expression for this biblical writer. The psalmist invokes God's past creative-salvific acts in order to inspire new ones in the present (a common pattern of lament psalms). And this recital homologizes 1) the mythic destruction of the Taninim and Leviathan in order to permit the ordering of creation (v. 13, 14; cf. Job 40, 41 and Isa 51); 2) the mythic creation of day and night, stars and sun, the yearly seasons in their regular temporal process (v. 16, 17; cf. Gen 1); and 3) the historical covenant designed not only as a contract between God and man but also including man's obligation to God to create a law-governed society on earth like that of David and Solomon (v. 20, 21; cf. Deut, Lev, etc.). And the covenant is symbolized by the ark that has come to rest in the Davidic kingdom (see Ps 132:8-12).

What ties together these various motifs in Ps 74 is the common metaphor of creation by establishing order, evident in the three instances cited above, expressed in both mythic (1, 2 above) and historical (3 above) modes. It is not the biblical writers and editors, but we ourselves today who seem to have the peculiar self-imposed task of needing to choose between these two as if they were mutually exclusive modes of truth. If we can fully accept them both as alternate and complementary modes of consciousness, affecting both experience and expression, perhaps such a choice will prove to be unnecessary in the future as it has been in the past.

IV

Resurrection in the New Testament is fully as central to the text, tradition, and faith as *creation* in the Old Testament. Just as there would have been no faith, or at least no Jewish tradition as it has come to be, without the creation of the kingdom of Israel, so also would there be no Christian faith as it has come to be without the crucifixion and resurrection of Jesus. And just as "God creates" was and is a symbolic statement expressing man's relation with God in a particular way, in the past and present, so is "He is risen" a symbolic statement expressing in another way man's relation with the transcendent in the future.[25]

Let us examine some representative passages where resurrection is the issue to see for ourselves once again the various ways in which this central symbolic statement has been expressed in the New Testament itself.

Empty Grave (Matt 28:6; Mark 16:6; Luke 24:3; John 20:15-18). This story from the gospels is familiar to every child and indeed appears to form the basis of man's faith in Jesus as himself the Lord and/or the unique son of God. The stone set before the sepulchre in which Jesus' dead body had been laid some days before has been rolled away and the grave is empty. Workmen, angels or (in the case of Luke) Jesus himself appear to announce to Mary and/or Mary Magdalene who have come that Jesus is risen from the dead as he had foretold. And it is the apparent claim to the historical, empirical validity of this account that has led Christians to base their faith on the literal truth of the apparently God-given absence of Jesus' physical body from his tomb. Its absence seems to prove that God raised him up to heaven.

It is clear, however, that even these accounts record no simple historical event.

In each case the women find an empty tomb and (with the exception of Mark) encounter and converse with angelic presences; in the case of Luke Jesus himself appears to them to explain what has happened. Is this history? Not in the modern sense, for supernatural beings intrude. These events are both literal and interpreted, both historic and mythic at the same time in these very accounts. One gets the feeling that for these women to see the empty tomb was instantly to believe in the reality of Jesus' resurrection because of their own expectation that this might happen.

On what was this expectation based? On Jesus' own words about himself, self-expectations which had been based on Old Testament prophetic utterances.[26] And perhaps also on other resurrection expectations present in current Jewish society that had existence largely outside of what came to be included in the biblical tradition, hints of which can be found in the present canonical text, and which are more expansively documented in the Apocryphal works.[27]

Jewish Resurrection Beliefs. Such beliefs are referred to importantly during Paul's trial (Acts 23:1-8) before his own people where he claims to be a Pharisee because he believes in the resurrection of the dead. In fact the very reason for his arrest is the annoyance of the opposing party of Jews, the Sadducees, who do not hold these beliefs, at Paul's "proclaiming in Jesus the resurrection from the dead." This resurrection is evidently an expectation which some Jews came to believe was fulfilled in Jesus himself. In the letters of the apostles, this identification and claim is made more explicit; the promise of "resurrection from the dead" or "eternal life" is a basic expectation and teaching of both Paul and John (see 1 Cor 15; Phil 3:10, 11; 1 Thes 4:13-17; Titus 1:2; John 1:1-3; 5:13, etc.).

Let us look at Paul's summary of the teaching about resurrection in 1 Cor 15. He goes to some lengths to explain the meaning of the statement that Jesus is risen. "But if there is no resurrection of the dead, then Christ has not been raised (v. 13). But in fact Christ has been raised from the dead, the first fruits of those who have fallen asleep" (v. 20). Paul seems to be substantiating an earlier doctrine by pointing to Christ's resurrection; he is saying that Christ's resurrection proves the truth of the earlier teaching that we all will be resurrected by God after our own apparent deaths. And furthermore, our physical body will be "raised a spiritual body" (v. 44) whose nature we cannot now understand. And the meaning of Christ's sacrifice was that his death and risenness made possible the resurrection of all (faithful) men. "For as in Adam all die, so also in Christ shall all be made alive. But each in his own order: Christ the first fruits, then at his coming, those who belong to Christ" (v. 22, 23).

What then was the substance of these Jewish resurrection hopes which Jesus appears to have fulfilled? There were evidently a number of such beliefs, made up of Old Testament prophetic expectations like the "day of the Lord" (Isa 2:21; 13:6, 9; 22:5; Jer 46:10; Joel 1:15; Amos 8:9; 9:11; Obad v. 15; Zeph 1:14, 15, etc.), the "suffering servant" (Isa 7:14; 9:6, 7; 42:1-4; 49:1-3; 52:13-15; 53:1-12), and the "son of man" (Dan 7:13; 8:15-17; 10:16, 18; 12:1; 12:1, 5-7); and other elements not found in the Old Testament. 1 Cor 15:51-54 strongly echoes the prophecies found in the book of Revelation, and it is only here in the New Testament that these Jewish resurrection hopes (and other expectations for the coming of God at the end of time) find clear and startling voice.

> Lo! I tell you a mystery. We shall not all sleep but we shall all be changed in a moment, in the twinkling of an eye, at the last trumpet. For the trumpet shall sound, and the dead will be raised imperishable (Rev 15:51, 52).

Rev 20 and 21 culminate a lengthy series of visions as to what will happen at the end of time when God comes again to earth in order to wipe out evil and to transform imperfection into perfection. The final events are presaged in 11:15:

> Then the seventh angel blew his trumpet, and there were loud voices in heaven saying, "The kingdom of the world has become the kingdom of our Lord and of his Christ, and he shall reign for ever and ever."

The historical realm has become illuminated, transformed by the presence of the transcendent: "then God's temple in heaven opened and the ark of his covenant was seen within his temple; and there were flashes of lightening, loud noises, peals of thunder, and earthquake, and heavy hail" (11:19). The holy of holies is at last revealed! And in ch. 21, the final day of the Lord brings a renewal of the whole of existence:

> Then I saw a new heaven and a new earth; for the first heaven and the first earth had passed away and the sea was no more. . . . and I heard a great voice from the throne saying, "Behold, the dwelling of God is with men. He will dwell with them, and they shall be his people, and God himself will be with them; he will wipe away every tear from their eyes, and death shall be no more . . . for the former things have passed away" (v. 1-4).

It is this collection of beliefs that God will come again to earth at the end of historic time (as he did in creation, exodus, Sinai, etc.) to bring eternal life to the faithful, to renew and transform all existence, that lies behind the Jewish acceptance of Jesus as the harbinger of these events through his own resurrection, the sign of the truth of these expectations. It is this that we see informing the theology of Paul.

Resurrection, in these teachings, is a symbolic statement whose content is the relationship between man and God, expected in future time. Phrases like "death shall be no more" (Rev 21:4), "night shall be no more" (Rev 22:5, cf. Isa 60:18-19) are mythical ways of describing this indescribable coming-together-ness when there will be no more need for a symbolic connection between known and unknown, between man and God, for all will be fully known; and the language itself that relates the two will be rendered unnecessary.[28] And this is pictured as the end of history as we know it now precisely because history is the realm of existence fully known to man but from which God appears to be absent. Paul's statement in 1 Corinthians conveys this clearly: "as in Adam all die" — men are condemned to historical existence and death — "so in Christ are all made alive" — so is eternal life, or the continual presence of God accessible to the faithful through Christ's resurrection.

What does this have to do with myth and history? As in the Old Testament, and the two are completely interfused in the teachings themselves, the coming of God at the end of history is analogous to God's creation of history at the beginning of the world (even the same images are used to describe it). God's presence to man is non-historic; history is equivalent to separation. As "creation" was a symbolic statement, mythically conveying the relationship between man and God (of dependence, obedience, and providence) in past and present, so is "resurrection" a symbolic statement of the future relationship between man and God. The empty tomb accounts of the gospel included both historical and mythic aspects, the empty tomb being an empirical event, the claim "he is risen" being an interpretation using mythical language, involving a supernatural referent. Likewise, the (Jewish) resurrection expectation of Paul, in the light of which he interprets Jesus, includes both historic and mythical aspects. Mythic in the description of God's defeat of the beasts of evil, the renewal of the earth, and the raising of the dead; and historical in that this is to occur after the passage of history but as the last event in history, in future time when time itself comes to a close. Again the two attitudes coincide in the telling of the events of the text.

Appearances to the Apostles (Matt 28:9, 16-20; Luke 24:13, 31, 36; John 20:19ff.; Acts 10:40, 41; 22:7-11; 26:14-18; 1 Cor 15:4-9; etc.). A third set of instances in which Jesus' resurrection is central emphasizes still another way of experiencing this symbolic truth. Paul summarizes these instances confessionally in 1 Cor 15:3-8:

> For I delivered to you as of first importance what I also received, that Christ died for our sins in accordance with the scriptures, that he was raised on the third day in accordance with the scriptures, and that he appeared to Cephas, then to the twelve. Then he appeared to more than five hundred brethren at one time, most of whom are alive, though some have fallen asleep. Then he appeared to James, then to all the apostles. Last of all, as to one untimely born, he appeared also to me.

In the gospels the first appearances of Jesus to the apostles occur shortly after Mary and/or Mary Magdalene view the empty tomb, in fact as a result of it: "On the evening of that day, the first day of the week, the doors being shut where the disciples were, for fear of the Jews, Jesus came and stood among them and said to them, 'Peace be with you' " (John 20:19). This and other instances of his appearance are given in Acts, for example in 10:40, 41: ". . . but God raised him on the third day and made him manifest; not to all the people but to us who were chosen by God as witnesses, who ate and drank with him after he rose from the dead." And of particular importance is the conversion of Paul as a direct result of seeing Jesus on the road to Damascus after his death (Acts 22:7-11; 26:14-18). It appears in fact to be these supernatural experiences of Jesus' presence after his crucifixion that 1) convinced the apostles that he was truly risen from the dead, in body, 2) demonstrated to them that they would also share in this eternal life (Rom 6:5: ". . . for if we have been united with him in a death like his, we shall certainly be united with him in a resurrection like his"), and 3) that galvanized them into action as united preachers of the word who despite all obstacles and persecutions continued to teach the meaning of Christ's resurrection to all men.

> We put no obstacle in any one's way, so that no fault may be found with our ministry, but as servants of God we commend ourselves in every way: through great endurance, in afflictions, hardships, calamities, beatings, imprisonments, tumults, labors, watching, hunger; by purity, knowledge, forbearance, kindness, the Holy Spirit, genuine love, truthful speech and the power of God; . . . (2 Cor 6:3-5)

How was this possible? In their own minds, by the activity of the Holy Spirit. Look again, for example, at John 20:19-23 where Jesus first appears to the apostles after his death:

> Jesus came and stood among them and said to them, "Peace be with you." When he said this, he showed them his hands and his side.... He breathed on them, and said to them, "Receive the Holy Spirit. If you forgive the sins of any, they are forgiven; if you retain the sins of any, they are retained."

What is this Holy Spirit, inspiring like the breath of God? If the experience of Jesus speaking to and eating with the apostles was indeed historical and empirical (see especially the events with doubting Thomas recorded in John 20:24-29), it was by this mythical doctrine of the Holy Spirit that the continued presence of Jesus among his followers was explained; it is a symbolic statement embodying a particular religious truth. The Holy Spirit is what relates man and God not in creation at the beginning of time, nor in resurrection of the body after death at the end of time, but in the very midst of time, in the experiencing of historical events. As Jesus himself knew in speaking to Thomas: "Have you believed because you have seen me? Blessed are those who have not seen and yet believe" (John 20:29). Both those who accept empirical evidence foremost, like Thomas and Paul, and those for whom the symbol suffices are included.

Again and again thereafter, countless times in Acts and in the letters of Peter, Paul, and John, it is the activity of the Holy Spirit that inspires, motivates, guides the apostles in their teachings and trials; it is by the Holy Spirit that their faith in God and Jesus Christ is maintained.[29] The Holy Spirit becomes the symbolic phrase for the inexpressible relationship between man and God manifest most vividly in Jesus himself and secondarily through the apostles. For example:

> And when they had prayed, the place in which they were gathered together was shaken; and they were all filled with the Holy Spirit and spoke the word of God with boldness (Acts 4:31).

> All who keep his commandments abide in him, and he in them. And by this we know that he abides in us, by the Spirit which he has given us (1 John 3:24).

In fact, Paul says: "... no one can say 'Jesus is Lord' except by the Holy Spirit" (1 Cor 12:3): In other words, acceptance of this particular symbolic statement of Jesus' God-hood is only possible by non-empirical means. That faith depends not on historical events alone but on their symbolic meaning was evident to Paul and apparently to other biblical writers as well. In other words, the modern crisis of historical consciousness was entirely unknown to these men as any sort of crisis for they never considered the empirical and symbolic views of events to be mutually exclusive. In both the Old and New Testaments God acts through history; man's relation with God is experienced and expressed symbolically in both mythic and historic modes, but it is the central symbols that lie at the heart of the faith that remain constant. The Holy Spirit is just such a central symbol, a symbolic way of saying that Jesus is risen and lives in us: just as in Gen 2:7, God's breathing into Adam's nostrils was a symbolic way of saying what can be explained discursively as the fact that man depends on God for his origin and sustenance. The unknown and the known, God and man, are related in both cases by *inspiration*, which is a biblical metaphor central to both testamental traditions. Does it matter whether these are primarily historical or mythical teachings? Not really. The modes of language are many; the central symbols that remain are the bases of faith.[30]

In summary, the symbolic teaching of "resurrection" in the New Testament can be seen to have been expressed in a number of different ways, in which the two modes of mythical and historical consciousness alternate and interrelate dynamically. The empty tomb, the future day of the Lord, and the appearance of Jesus to the apostles all have empirical, historical aspects. They also bear mythic components. "He is risen," "eternal life," and the "Holy Spirit" are all non-empirical, symbolic statements whose purpose is to express the otherwise inexpressible relationship between man and God, between known and unknown dimensions of existence, in the only way possible — symbolic language. "Resurrection" in the New Testament, like "creation" in the Old, can be seen to be a basic statement of a symbolic nature central to the faith that has been both experienced and expressed through modes of consciousness both historical and mythic, these being congenially complementary to the writers of the Bible themselves.

V

What are the bases of faith today? It seems more appropriate to attempt to identify certain metaphors as symbolic statements basic to faith, such as creation and resurrection as indicated in the previous sections, than to choose which of the several accounts or modes in which these appear is the correct one to the exclusion of others. Through our brief study of certain biblical passages we have seen that myth and history can be understood as complementary modes of consciousness through which these central metaphors have been expressed. In fact it may be that the content of what we call revelation lies not in any specific empirical or historical data, but that it is these central symbolic statements or connective links between man and God (conscious and unconscious, known and unknown, right- and left-brain functions) that are precisely that which is revealed in revelation. These statements are then endlessly unpacked throughout the ongoing tradition because their non-empirical pole taps an exhaustless source (God, the unconscious, or whatever you choose to call it).

To summarize, let us define *history* as a linear mode of experience and expression that relates primarily to the left-brain analytic mode of consciousness. It is from that dimension of man's psyche that is in constant relationship with what we call the external, empirical world, although the true relationship is probably closer to what von Franz is describing when she depicts psyche and matter, mind and world, as two poles of a single continuum (see note 14 above). And let us define *myth* as a synthetic mode of experience and expression that derives from the right-brain, holistic mode of consciousness. It relates to that part of man's psyche that is largely inaccessible to the external empirical world, is largely non-verbal, and is more closely in touch with the repository of inarticulate, instinctual patterns, or archetypes, that affect external life indirectly through symbolic activity but are not directly accessible to consciousness.

Symbolic activity is manifest as a synthesis of right- and left-brain functions, both in experience itself and in the expression of that experience, which may take verbal or bodily form, a natural and necessary human psychic function. Both knowledge and meaning involve the entire psyche, both holistic and analytic functions, both inner mythic and outer historical dimensions of existence. And it is through symbolic activity that congruence between the two is effected. *Myth* and *history* describe these two modes of consciousness as found in every man's life as ways of experiencing, thinking, and expressing. They can be readily discerned in the Bible as complementary ways of expressing the central symbols of faith which themselves are metaphors relating these two functions in the first place. Man and world derive from and depend on God. Likewise, the religious tradition derives from and depends on its own basic symbols and myth and history as modes of expression which are similarly interdependent.[31]

The problem of the modern world with respect to myth and history is that a too exclusive dependence on the historical mode of consciousness in recent years has effected a disruption of the biblical view of the world to the degree that its mythic dimensions are being rejected entirely in favor of empirically verifiable, historically accurate verities which have come to be considered truer than myth. The situation today is what has been described as one of "broken myth" in which the power of myth as myth, understood to be exclusive truth, over men has been broken. It is a time in which Christians, both those of erstwhile simple faith and theologians alike find it difficult to accept the non-empirical bases of their faith, precisely because of the almost exclusive cultural acceptance of history as the revealer of truth in comparison with which myth is deemed false. Instead of "God is dead" we really mean "the old myth is broken." Need this mean the end of faith? I think not.

If we can, as this essay suggests, realize that for ourselves today as for the writers of the Bible, myth and history may be experienced as complementary modes of consciousness influencing both our experience and its expression, then we may begin to revalue our own mythic traditions. And if biblical myths are now "broken" for us, we can nevertheless continue to appropriate these myths for our own lives precisely because of their symbolic character.[32] *It is not the literal contents of the myth but its central symbols that in fact form the content of revelation.* The specific contents of myths and the actual historical circumstances of the tradition change from age to age through time; only the symbols remain.[33]

The value of myth, however "broken," lies in that it may be a continuing source of revelation even when it is not believed literally as the complete and only truth. Von Franz provides insight into the nature of broken and unbroken myth when she describes the state of "archaic identity" (Lévy-Bruhl's "participation mystique") as a state of non-difference between the unconscious psyche and the outer world; cosmic reality and man's mind are undifferentiated. Myth is broken when a distinction between inner and outer is consciously made, when there is distinguished a difference between the world of a particular religious world-view and the world of empirical perception. As Stevenson says, this is the situation today in the Western world, when man "may cosmicize his world apart from myth," and usually does, at least apart from the traditional Jewish and Christian views of the world.[34] Yet broken myths maintain their power, not any longer as absolute truths but, as Dupré says, as "means for religious reflection . . . [Their] polyvalent richness continues to feed religious reflection" precisely because of their transcendent referents, their symbolic nature. And I would say that the potential of broken myth goes much further than this, that to know myth as symbol is not to deprive it of its meaning, but to begin in a new way to appropriate the continuing power of symbol as symbol to inspire, enrich, and inform one's life with continually new insight. And I would conclude further that this process can be as true of history as of myth, for both are symbolic modes of expression. It will be necessary, then, to recognize the value of symbol as symbol in both myth and history, rather than to try to reduce either to another mode of thought.

What, finally, does this point of view contribute to our understanding of biblical traditions? Historical circumstances alter from age to age, language styles replace one another successively through time, but the basic symbols which are not necessarily wedded to any one historical era, nor to any single form of linguistic expression, being in their nature partly non-verbal, remain. What is the locus of the source of continuing revelation in the biblical traditions? It consists of the basic metaphors, disclosed but not exhausted, in the text itself. Two of these, creation and resurrection, continue to lie at the basis of faith and life for much of the Western world today. Whether or not men are self-consciously "religious," these central metaphors continue to inform their lives. In such pervasive ways do religious symbols influence entire cultural traditions.

These central symbolic statements will no doubt continue to lie at the bases of biblical faith, taking new forms from age to age, in both historical and mythic modes, and probably in other modes as well. History and myths both have contents limited to particular times and places and cultural milieus; but the symbols upon which both are based, relating always the known to the unknown, are illimitable, and will continue to nurture man's faith as long as it needs nurturing. There is really nothing to fear in the current "crisis," for "Behold the dwelling of God is with men . . . and there shall be neither mourning nor crying nor pain any more." The source of life is, whatever symbolic language is used to describe it, truly inexhaustible and ever available to man.

NOTES

[1]For a discussion of different ways the term history is used, see W. T. Stevenson, "Myth and the Crisis of Historical Consciousness," collected in this volume.

[2]M.-L. von Franz, *Patterns of Creativity Mirrored in Creation Myths* (Zurich: Spring Publications, 1972), p. 5.

[3]Louis Dupré, *The Other Dimension* (New York: Doubleday & Company, Inc., 1972), pp. 221, 225, 226. The symbolic or transcendental nature of religious language may be maintained whether or not the "hidden" referent of a symbol is objectively real; whether or not God exists need not be resolved in order to grasp the way religious language functions in men's lives.

[4]See note 1.

[5]J. Needleman, A. K. Bierman, and J. A. Gould, *Religion for a New Generation* (New York: Macmillan Company, 1973), pp. 478-79.

[6]It seems to me that, despite his disclaimer, this is precisely what Bultmann himself has done. In claiming to reinterpret biblical truths "existentially" he has identified a cluster of basic metaphors which despite his non-supernatural language, are still symbolic. For example, the phrase "radical openness to the future" places the unknown in future time, transcendence being temporally defined rather than spatially (the old man with the white beard up there in the sky being passé), but Bultmann's temporal phrase is still symbolic, or mythical in nature. His use of the terms "kerygma," "cross," "faith," etc. are similarly symbolic/mythic simply because their content can never be entirely reduced to existential terms if existential means by definition non-transcendent and if they are key terms in a particular religious tradition. See Richard Ray, "Is Eliade's Metapsychoanalysis an End Run around Bultmann's Demythologizing?", collected in this volume, for a discussion of this aspect of Bultmann's thought.

[7]R. Ornstein, *The Psychology of Consciousness* (San Francisco: W. H. Freeman & Company, 1972), pp. 51-53.

[8]Ornstein, *Consciousness*, pp. 58-59.

[9]Ornstein, *Consciousness*, p. 69.

[10]See Ornstein, *Consciousness*, pp. 58-61 for summaries of experiments performed with split-brain people; see also p. 73 for further reading suggestions on this issue.

[11]Stevenson, "Myth and the Crisis," p. 8.

[12]Dupré, *Other Dimension*, p. 242.

[13]Adam, 4004 B.C.

[14]Von Franz, *Creation Myths*, p. 242.

[15]Von Franz, *Creation Myths*, p. 8.

[16]Stevenson, "Myth and the Crisis," p. 15.

[17]I do not mean to suggest that this script is unalterable, nor that such meanings and patterns do not also develop later in life (religious conversion amounts to an abrupt and radical change in life-script), but rather that early childhood experiences, being the first, are the most powerful in the formation of basic symbolic patterns. People differ greatly in the tenacity with which these early patterns are maintained; both conservative and liberal attitudes in this regard are to be found in every cultural and religious tradition.

[18]Dupré, *Other Dimension*, p. 268.

[19]Dupré, *Other Dimension*, p. 312.

[20]It is our own dogged and exclusive adherence to the analytic, linear, historical point of view that demands of us again and again that *we decide* which came first. I am trying to suggest that even this sort of chronological question may be the wrong sort of question to ask, even as I ask it, of the text or of life, if it is the only sort of question we know how to ask.

[21]Note later in the text in the Deuteronomic view of history, that the same model is assumed, that man's material prosperity results from his maintaining an orderly relationship with God, namely the obligations of the covenant.

[22]Note that in the previous story the commandment was to be fruitful; here it is to obey. These appear to be variations on a theme which are combined in the covenant, cf. note 21 above.

[23]Note how the later lessons of Israel's historical experience, in the monarchy and in exile, at least according to the prophetic interpreters, have been seen in terms of this same metaphor. Just as Adam disobeyed God and was thrust out, so did Israel disobey God in the Davidic kingdom, and as a result was cast into exile. Again can we say, need we decide, which is prior, the exile or this creation myth? They explain, express, interpret each other, non-chronologically. The mythic and historic views illuminate a metaphor common to both.

[24]The biblical metaphor is identical; it is only our modern way of thinking, our modern terminology, that forces a linguistic distinction to be made between creation and salvation (and providence as well). These are temporal distinctions originally largely irrelevant to the basic symbolic statement that God saves/creates/provides.

[25]Would there have been any Christian faith if Jesus had not been crucified? I believe there would have been both faith and a religious tradition based on the life of the man Jesus, but it would have found different basic symbols other than that of resurrection central to the faith. It was, in my opinion, the impact of the personality of Jesus, fully open as he was (and as we are not) to the transcendent through himself, that inspired a resonant faith in the hearts and minds of his followers. His death was the occasion of the formation of a powerful symbolic way of viewing the relationship between God and man, but not the only symbolic activity of his life. A Christian faith would probably have come to be, based on a different set of symbols than those which have in fact come to be central.

[26]Hos 5:15—6:3; 13:14; Isa 52:13-53; 26:13-19; Ezek 34:23, 24; 37:1-14, 24-28; Dan 12:2-3; see also Job 14; 19:23-29; and Ps 16:9-11; 49:13-20; 73:23-28; 88; 116:1-11; 118:15-18.

27 2 Macc 7:9, 14, 23, 29; Wis 2:12—6:11; Jub 23:30, 31; Enoch 22:3; 38:1-6; 62:1-16; 91:8-11; Judah 25:1; Zeb 10; Ben 10:6; 2 Bar 30:1; 4 Ezra 7:27, 32-42; Ps Sol 3:9-12; 14:8-10.

28 Just as in the prediction of Jer 31:33: the law written on men's hearts will replace the external obligations of the covenant.

29 Acts 2:1-4, 38; 4:31-33; 5:32; 13:9, 52; 15:8; 19:6; Rom 5:5; 1 Cor 12:3; 2 Cor 3:17; Titus 3:5, 6; 2 Pet 1:20, 21; 1 John 3:24; Rev 1:10; 4:2; etc.

30 For example, even if I interpret the trinity in psychological terms, it is not thereby reduced to psychology; the mystery remains. *God* names the indescribable but powerful unconscious, the non-empirical dimension of human existence; *Jesus*, the man, represents the empirical, historical dimension of existence; *Christ* is a symbolic term for the dynamic relationship between God and Jesus through the person of Jesus, or unconscious and conscious aspects of oneself; the *Holy Spirit* is a symbolic term for the possibility of this dynamic in all men. In the Christian tradition, if the Age of Faith dwelt on God, the Age of Reason focused on Jesus the man, perhaps we today are living in the Age of Symbol when the Holy Spirit may speak through us all (cf. Jer 31:33, 34).

31 Notice how even in my interpretation of myth and history in the Bible I am using these same biblical metaphors in my own thinking. If my argument appears to be circular, then it has demonstrated its point. My standpoint is still from within the tradition for my metaphors come from it.

32 On "broken myth" see "Myth and the Mystery of the Future," by Lee W. Gibbs, collected in this volume.

33 For instance, this is why the three-story universe with God as an old man with a white beard sitting on his throne in the sky are images passing away, no longer central to faith. They are the literal contents of a myth whose symbol otherwise remains, albeit in different dress (for example: Bultmann's "radical openness to the future" may be replacing "God in the sky on a throne" as a statement of transcendence). This is also why the dietary laws of Leviticus and the New Testamental injunctions against sex and the secondary place of women may also be rejected in the modern view as characteristic of particular historical and social conditions of the past that no longer obtain and are considered practices no longer central to faith. The central symbols, however, still remain.

34 The question remains: is a re-cosmicization by definition a re-mythicization? How mythic in fact is Western science?

Is Eliade's Metapsychoanalysis an End Run Around Bultmann's Demythologization?

Richard A. Ray

WESTERN man has been involved in the critical discovery of myth for quite a while. The process has been going on at least since the time of Xenophanes (565-470 B.C.), who took it upon himself to reject the mythological accounts of the gods he had inherited from Homer and Hesiod.[1] In a comparable way, Upanishadic culture had focused a critical eye on the myths of India. The results of both of these demythicization processes have proven to be incalculable. As a result, the mythologies could no longer represent for the elites of these cultures what they had represented for their forefathers. In spite of the development of these critical perspectives, however, the fact remains that after twenty-five cenuries of critical reflection, the grip of the ancient myths on the imagination is still quite powerful. While our view of myths is far different from that of our forefathers, our appreciation of both the mysterious appeal of mythic lore and our continuing proclivity to think in mythical forms is deepening.

The nineteenth century saw the beginning of a new era in the critical appraisal of myth. The brothers Jacob and Wilhelm Grimm illustrated in their *Deutsche Mythologie* the abundance of living mythic materials in contemporary European peasant cultures. Andrew Lang saw in these and other traditions the evidence of the continuing development from primitive stages into further forms of civilization. Freud and Jung, on the other hand, found in myths the imaginative display of unconscious psychic forces. Although Freud's emphasis on the struggle of the individual to grow to maturity in the complexity of the emotional forces of the nuclear family remains influential, Jung's concern with the endurance of the psychological heritage or archetypes through the generations has persisted in stimulating scholars in diverse fields.

Among those who have shown the most dexterity and creativity in carrying Jung's work further are Mircea Eliade and Joseph Campbell. In this essay we will look primarily at the writings of Eliade, for he has attempted to appropriate the Jungian concern with archetypes for the Christian tradition. Campbell, on the other hand, has pursued the constructive capacity of the human mind to be shaped by and to reshape the mythic inheritants of diverse cultures. In a sense the streams of both scholars flow closely by one another, and the creative interplay of their perspectives will provide an enormously interesting field of research for succeeding scholars.

In Eliade's writings, in particular, we find a persistent attempt to identify the religious aspects of myth. As a critical scholar he does not take the narrative face value of the myths literally. The dimension of the religious is not found in a slavish attempt to literalize or historicize the myths. Instead, he looks for the archetypal form which is expressed in the myths. These forms are then seen by Eliade as providing the clue to the religious element in our own lives today. Eliade thus suggests, somewhat as did Tillich, that lying within both the myths and ourselves are the psychic keys to religious renewal.

Eliade sees a great paradox in our perspectives about ourselves. While we are far more indebted to mythologies of past cultures and much more involved with mythic forms of imagination than we recognize, we increasingly think of ourselves in secular terms. Eliade indicates our unique historical self-consciousness when he notes that "modern man's originality, his newness in comparison with traditional societies, lies precisely in his determination to regard himself as a purely historical being, in his wish to live in a basically desacralized cosmos."[2] In his self-understanding, modern man has lost touch with the element of the sacred. The Christian faith fails to carry an experience of the sacred to us because we are inclined to view even the symbols of the faith itself as elements in a historical and secular landscape. We cannot even glimpse the bearing of sacred reality on our lives in our heritage of myths and symbols. Eliade holds out the hope, however, that we may once again recognize the presence of the sacred. By entering into dialogue with the myths of remote cultures, we may learn to recognize the sacred which, unknown to us, touches our lives in profound ways. Our lives, Eliade writes, abound in mythic fragments which may be rejuvenated, "the life of modern man is swarming with half-forgotten myths, decaying hierophanies, and secular symbols . . . a quantity of mythological litter still lingers in the ill-controlled zones of the mind."[3] We can rediscover the reality of the sacred in our lives by bringing the religious perspective of the great mythic cultures to illumine this enduring mythological activity which is obscure to us. Thus Eliade does not attempt to demythologize religious tradition. Instead he looks for the religious expression in the myths and their historical transformations. The myths themselves as well as the mythic forms expressed unconsciously in our thoughts or actions provide clues to the religious meaning of both past and present experience. Accordingly, it is Eliade's emphasis on the pervasive potential of mythic thought in our psychic lives which offers new possibilities for those who look wistfully at the symbolism of their religious tradition.

Our interest is to delineate the broad beams in the structure of Eliade's approach to myth. Because Eliade has so far presented his ideas in thematic essays and anthologies, a summary of his thought may serve as an introduction to it. In addition, a brief comparison of his methodology with that of Rudolph Bultmann may help to raise some continuing issues for critical study. This essay is divided into five areas. The first concerns Eliade's understanding of the structure of myth and its place in religious revelation. The second focuses on the *function* of myth and symbolism in our knowledge of both the self and God. The third brings together the elements in Eliade's view of the distinctive form or morphology of the Christian faith. The fourth demonstrates Eliade's attempt to identify the prevalent mythic structures in contemporary secular ideas. And the fifth offers some indication of the promise of Eliade's phenomenology of religious forms for a revival of theology and a rediscovery of the vitality of the Christian faith.

I

Eliade does not define religious experience or revelation explicitly. Perhaps wisely, he does not, as R. D. Baird has pointed out, begin with a definition of any religious phenomena at all.[4] Nevertheless, Eliade has not ignored the need to describe the distinctive characteristics of myth. It is his description of these unique characteristics which indicates both the structure of myth and its place in revelation.

Eliade recognizes that myths have multiple sources. The activity of the natural cycles of the seasons makes a fundamental contribution. The impact of significant historical events in the cultural memory adds important ingredients. But the creative act which brings to expression the myth itself is the contribution of the human imagination. He writes in *Patterns of Comparative Religion* that "myth is an autonomous act of creation by the mind: it is through that act of creation that revelation is brought about — not through the things or events it makes use of."[5] Eliade continues in the same place to illustrate the way the mind finds in a natural event the prototype model of the form of a myth.

> Only myth can transform this event into a *mode of being*: on the one hand, of course, because the death and resurrection of the vegetation gods became archetypes of all deaths and all resurrections, whatever form they take, and on whatever plane they occur, but also because they are better than any empirical or rational means of revealing human destiny.[6]

In *Myths, Dreams, and Mysteries*, we find that Eliade adds another emphasis in his description of myth.[7] Here, as well as in other books, Eliade is concerned to identify the special *content* of myths which make them different from other stories. He describes myths as containing the revelation of the narrative of the uniquely creative and exemplary events that occurred before time began. Myths tell how things were first made. They tell how either the cosmos as a whole or some part of it, such as a plant or a significant institution or ritual, were created. Myths give the dramatic account of the Supernatural Beings who accomplished the primordial, creative breakthrough. These actions of the Supernaturals were decisive in human existence, in that they determined its basic structure. They indicated what a human being essentially is and what the right and proper actions of his life should be. These creative actions by the gods are the only ones which are truly real. All other attitudes, experiences, and actions are undeniably transient. They fade away. The original events, however, are lasting. Moreover, they can and should be repeated in rituals and initiation experiences, for as man repeats them he invokes the events which are truly real and brings them into his own existence. "Every myth, whatever its nature, recounts an event that took place *in illo tempore*, and constitutes as a result, a precedent and pattern for all the actions and situations later to repeat that event."[8] Myths thus preserve the memory of the originating and exemplary events. And by recollection and re-enactment of this memory people are able to participate in the divine acts of creation. They become contemporaries of the gods. In traditional or primitive cultures this re-enactment is not seen as an accessory or luxury for a basically meaningful life. It is not thought to "add" a second dimension of meaning to life, as contemporary liturgies are sometimes regarded in modern secular culture. The re-enactments of the creative events in traditional cultures are fundamental because they are seen as the only spiritual way to survive the ravages and destructions of time. All else is transient and passing. As the myths are repeated they are "lived," and the celebrants in the ritual are "seized by the sacred, exalting power of the events recollected or re-enacted."[9] This ritual of re-enactment imaginatively preserves the order of the world. It thus protects the world from collapsing into chaos with the passage of time. The ritual thus "transforms 'chaos' into the 'cosmos' and, therefore, renders human existence possible — prevents it, that is, from regression to the level of zoological existence."[10]

It is important that myth and ritual are rooted in a sacred reality which exists prior to time. This structural rootedness gives myth the capacity to determine the nature of human existence. As it is remembered and re-enacted the dramatic recital of essential events and supernatural figures becomes a revelatory sequence. It reveals that which is neither illusory nor evanescent — that which should be called the "sacred" — as well as the structural relationship of the sacred to human life. Myth thus becomes part of a revelatory complex which includes the motifs of the original structure of the cosmos, the deterioration of the cosmos through time, and the religious resolution of the ensuing personal crises.

> On the one hand, the sacred is supremely the *other* than man — the transpersonal, the transcendent — and on the other hand, the sacred is the exemplary in the sense that it establishes patterns to be followed: by being transcendent and exemplary it compels the religious man to come out of personal situations to surpass the contingent and the particular and to comply with general values, with the universal.[11]

The exemplary strength and influence of the original archetypal actions thus provide the means for the resolution of personal as well as cosmic crises. As we discover something profound about ourselves, we find that deep within our own nature we are homologous to these basic actions. Our psychic structure is thus mysteriously related to the mythological events which give order and meaning to the cosmos. The revelation of this insight about ourselves assures us that there is more to our lives than our individual experiences. At the depths of our lives we encounter universal characteristics which are present in the structure of the universe as well as in the lives of all people at all times in history. Whatever personal crises we enter, we may also be aware that the universal character of our lives will endure. The celebrant who recognizes these universal characteristics through myth and ritual enters into the primal time of these creative events. He shares the enduring presence and immortality of the Supernaturals. Through the magic looking glass of myth he embraces a "magico-religious time which has no connection with succession in the true sense but forms the 'eternal now' of mythical time."[12]

II

In almost any situation, the functions of myths and symbols are deeply interrelated. This is particularly true for Eliade's perspective. As Robert

Leeyster says, "Myth for Eliade is that form of thought based upon symbols."[13] Symbols differ from myth, however, in the sense that they precede language and reason. However, as components of myths, they arise from the same conditions and structures. Like myths, they arise as the psyche encounters and adds further value to the seasonal changes of the natural world. "Opening" the natural object to additional meaning, symbols bring to light "hidden modalities of being."[14] For the primitive person nature is continually a kratophany or hierophany. It is a revelatory presence: it is never simply physical earth, sky and sea, however ugly or beautiful nature might seem in itself.

Containing an inherent logic of their own, symbols are not interpreted easily. They have no single references.[15] Rather, they have many meanings. They are multivalent, and as they pass through a society's history even more meanings become associated with them. Symbols are thus transformed by historical accretions. In spite of these multivalences, the power of the original archetypal models remain, and, indeed, even eventually reassert themselves. As Eliade puts it, the archetype "tends to disengage itself from its conditions in time and space and to become universal."[16] Thus for Eliade the pure archetypal, religious structure of a symbol largely controls its career through its cultural adaptations and associations. Because the symbolic archetypes endure in myths, men are liberated from the tyranny of transcience as they recall and live these archetypal elements.

Eliade's association with Jungian psychology is evident in his discussions of archetypes. Although he does not embrace Jung's views in respect to the origin of religion in the unconscious memory, he does accept Jung's general thesis that symbols can reappear spontaneously because they, or something that produces them, exist as memories in the unconscious.[17] Even when myths become corrupted into epic legends, ballads, customs, superstitions, etc., the archetypes within them remain creative and eventually reassert themselves. Understandably, Eliade does not elaborate on the origins of the archetypes in the psyche. He does, however, write that "man, whatever else he may be free of, is forever the prisoner of his own archetypal intuitions, formed at the moment when he first perceived his position in the cosmos."[18]

Myths and symbols are difficult to interpret not only because they are multivalent but also because they really constitute a language which is *sui generis*, distinct from all others. Eliade's understanding of the distinct ontological being of the sacred inevitably leads to this understanding of myth. John B. Cobb expresses Eliade's view of the ontological significance of myth for language very succinctly in the course of arguing against this general position. Cobb writes:

> If the Christian faith apprehends a reality radically different from all other reality, even to the extent that the term 'reality' cannot be used univocally, then the language of faith must be *sui generis*. We may assign the term 'myth' to such *sui generis* language.[19]

I believe that Eliade would agree with this statement.

As a language appropriate to an ontologically distinct reality, myth and symbol must be understood on their own terms. Thus, Eliade develops a mythological hermeneutic. This hermeneutic can be contrasted directly with Bultmann's effort to interpret myths in the New Testament on the conceptual model of existentialism. In place of Bultmann's appeal to Heidegger's thought for the conceptual vehicle, Eliade relies upon the comprehensive body of myths to provide an interpretive framework. Moreover, he believes that myths and symbols cannot be deciphered by comparing them with similar motifs in a single cultural epoch. They can be understood only when compared with similar symbolic forms as broadly as possible. Thus he writes in *The Two and The One* that "One cannot understand the significance of even a given type of Cosmic Tree until one has studied the most important types and variants."[20]

This survey of variant forms of the symbol, however, should be complimented by an analysis and comparison of the meanings of the particular forms. The result is not only the discovery of the significance of a specific symbol, such as the meaning of the Cosmic Tree in Mesopotamia or the Cross of Christ in Christianity, but also the isolation of the archetypal significance which had been hidden in every variant. The universal is thus recognized as present in the particular. The point is that the process is one of integration rather than reduction. Both the symbol's variant functions in different myths and its special role in each myth contributes to its meaning. Eliade writes: "One compares and contrasts two expressions of a symbol not in order to reduce them to a single pre-existent expression, but in order to discover the process by which a structure is capable of enriching its meaning."[21]

This method of comparison and analysis is the basic hermeneutical principle to follow in understanding a symbol's function and meaning. However, it is not to be followed at the expense of other kinds of information. In *Images and Symbols*, Eliade includes such disciplines as ethnology, depth psychology, and sociology in the comparative method.

Calling this pursuit a new *maieutics*, Eliade writes that it brings forth new thoughts and previously uncovered experiences. Somewhat similar to Socrates' approach in the *Theaetetus*, it delivers more information than we knew was held within us. Thus, this maieutics promises to make possible new depth of personal inwardness and the potential for a new human existence. As we would inherit new spiritual riches from this encounter with our inward, archaic selves, we would become new persons. We would be far more authentic, complete, and unrepressed than we are now.

The most comprehensive term which Eliade coins for this new hermeneutics is *metapsychoanalysis*.

> We have dared to use the term metapsychoanalysis because what is in question here is a more spiritual technique, applicable to elucidating the theoretical content of the symbols and archetypes, giving transparency and coherence to what is allusive, cryptic or fragmentary.[22]

The practice of this spiritual technique will result in more than an increase in objective data about human nature. As understanding about human life deepens it will result in a "new humanism'" with the accompaniment of fresh attitudes, beliefs, and behavior.[23] The function of symbols and myths is thus the clarification, in the final analysis, of the meaning of "wholeness" in life. The person who integrates the attitudes and perceptions found in the archaic myths with the technical and scientific sophistication of contemporary cultures will know what it means to be whole. Until we seek this integration we will not understand the ultimate function of symbols, for symbols and myths are produced as well as received by the whole person. Neither reason nor imagination, apart from this personal wholeness, serves to elucidate the meaning of myths.[24]

The interplay of symbol and myth in the evolution of personal wholeness is well illustrated by the symbol of the cosmogony. This symbol is of fundamental importance. As Eliade writes in *The Sacred and the Profane*, "The creation of the world becomes the archetype of every creative human gesture whatever its plane of reference might be."[25] A familiar example of the cosmogonic symbolism is found in the traditional coronation ceremony of the new king or pharaoh. Here the motif of the re-creation of order and stability in society is profoundly and often elaborately displayed by a ritual re-enactment of the cosmogony. The chaos of the leaderless society is overcome. So also a medicine man or a shaman heals his client of both spiritual and physical distress by symbolically invoking a new creation of the world. Through the function of symbol and myth, the celebrants in both cases are attempting to draw on the creative energy that was involved in the original cosmogony. In these, and even more common instances such as the dedication of a new home by a family, the function of the symbol is to provide a temporary access to the primordial time of creativity.[26]

The archetype of the cosmogony has, however, a dark as well as a light side to it. Before every creation there is a period of unformed chaos which is a symbolic equivalent of death. The seasonal death and rebirth of nature made this relation unavoidable for the primitive. The periodic transformations of the natural world thus provided a natural model for man to use in understanding his life and his relation to cosmic and national renewal. As Eliade writes,

> Every ritual repetition of the cosmogony is preceded by a symbolic regression to chaos . . . all the rites of rebirth or resurrection, and the symbols that they imply, indicate that the novice has attained to another mode of existence, inaccessible to those who have not undergone the initiatory ordeals, who have not tasted death.[27]

The symbol of the center is also unusually important. For primitives the center, whether its focus be a sacred space, an altar, a mountain, a tree, the navel of the earth, a tent pole, etc., is the axis of communication among the three levels of earth, heaven, and the underworld. The establishment of the center is thus a highly creative part of the cosmicization, of the attempt to bring order out of chaos. Like the cosmogony, the symbolism of the center is universal. Eliade writes that "every human being tends, even unconsciously, towards the Centre, and toward his own centre where he can find integral reality-sacredness."[28]

Initiation is likewise a motif which is found everywhere. It is a particularly sensitive structure of rite and myth, for it frequently relates the symbols of death and resurrection to the personal crises of the individual. In these rites the individual confronts the terrible realities of maturation, societal integration, death, and sexuality — along with the revelation of the divine. Initiation, whether of the adolescent or of the shaman, is regarded as a step beyond the natural, innocent existence of childhood into a mode of life which is open to spiritual realities.[29] It is symbolically expressed as a new birth or as a death and resurrection.

> Everywhere we have found the symbolism of death as the ground of all spiritual birth — that is, of regeneration. In all these contexts death signifies the surpassing of the profane, non-sanctified condition, the condition of the 'natural man,' ignorant of religion and blind to the spiritual."[30]

Initiation thus symbolizes a death to one form of existence and a rebirth to another. So also in Yoga and Buddhism one dies to profane time and is resurrected into the extra-sensory, unconditioned time of the absolute being.[31] There is also a converse effect of the relation between these symbols of spiritual transformation. The experience of initiation reflects back on the meaning of death and redefines it. From the primitive perspective, death is revalorized. Death is sacralized so that it represents the beginning of a new existence or the supreme initiation.[32]

Other variants of the symbols of death and resurrection are also related to rebirth or the creation of new life. The motif of the descent into the underworld and the ensuing battle with the forces of death for the sake of another is almost universal. It appears in Orpheus' search for Eurydice, the descent of the Indian Queen Mayanomati into Hell in quest of her husband's soul, and in the shaman's trance in which he searches for a lost soul.[33] In the concept of human sacrifice, death is pictured in terms of a seed which dies in the earth in order to reappear in an abundance of new forms. Even when this configuration of symbols includes the violent murder of a divinity, the death is understood as creative. When it is re-enacted its transforming power is present in the ritual as well as in living forms which spring from the immolated deity.[34]

Countless other symbols and myths, such as the nostalgia for paradise, the image of light, the *coincidentia oppositorum*, etc. could be correlated with death and resurrection or with the basic cosmogonic myth. Symbols thus are far from exclusive. They interlock and mutually illumine their values and meanings. The pervasive reach of mythic symbolism into the natural processes of life corresponds with Eliade's thesis that every person carries within himself a large body of the mythic reality of prehistoric societies. This profound involvement of myth in man's psychic crises also suggests the importance of Eliade's basic belief that symbols reveal a deeper, religious aspect of life than is immediately self-evident or that can be expressed in any other way.[35]

III

Eliade's understanding of the uniqueness of the Jewish and Christian complex of symbolism is ultimately based upon his distinction between the *deus otiosus*, the high God who creates and then abandons the earth, and the fecundative divinities who are modeled on the forces of nature. Because this supreme being withdraws, sometimes leaving the completion of the creation to his "son" or representative, he has had little representation in cults or temples. On the other hand, when he disappears, myths and rituals involving nature-oriented divinities flourish.[36] While we become preoccupied with these symbols of generative power, a "memory" of the supreme God survives in a camouflaged form. This cultural memory reappears in the surviving myths of cosmogony, a primordial paradise, the center of the world, the ascension, etc. In times of crises, when the fecundative powers of nature are seen as incompetent, we look beyond these deities to the renewed historical or natural cosmogony that only the high God can bring. In the myths, we then "remember" the high God. Even in more complacent times, strongly directed religious personalities can encounter the supreme deity in the distorted forms of the symbolism and lead to a renewal of community religious experience.[37]

Eliade feels that Yahweh originally confronted man as the high creative God. He did not appear in the succeeding epiphanies of the mystery of procreation and fertility. Nor was his worship directed toward maintaining an unceasing flow of vital energy. Rather, he addressed humans directly and "spiritually," summoning a worship which became interiorized. As Eliade puts it, "The religious forces set in motion by Yahweh are spiritual forces." Yahweh revealed himself in the form of a person who was present in history, and who called forth an interior worship in the form of faith.[38] Acting in history and addressing human beings, the divine expresses his complete freedom in being incarnate in Jesus Christ. History rather than cosmos becomes the supreme theophany. This radical revelation breaks the circular perspective of the death and renewal of the cosmos, and it thereby inaugurates the experience of time and history as meaningful and as linear. This experience, however, raises new questions about particular events. In a history in which certain events have become theophanies, and certain remain mute and secular, the Jew and the Christian encounter a profound theological challenge. They cannot reject all of history because the divine is revealed in it; but neither can they blindly embrace it all. In writing of the Christian, Eliade says, "He has continually to choose, to try to distinguish, in the tangle of historical events, the event which *for him* may be charged with a saving significance."[39] Entering into this "terrifying dialogue" with God, the Hebrew prophets regarded historical calamities as "negative theophanies" in which man was reconciled with God. Distinct from nature, God demanded what he wished of his people, paradoxically revealing the abyss between himself and mankind as well as offering a new relationship of faithful obedience. Even when this new relation was overtly accepted, man ignored the historic theophanies and sought satisfaction by focusing on ritual fault that could be corrected liturgically or sacrificially.[40]

Eliade holds that the theophany in Christ is unique in that the divine Incarnation has overcome the dissipation of profane time. By filling the historic time with the divine time of Christ's life, God has endowed history with being and meaning. Eliade turns his account apparently in the opposite direction, however, when he describes the final, eschatological deliverance as the complete abolition of history. Is Eliade inconsistent at this point? Thomas Altizer thinks so.[41] How could Eliade's view that the reality of the divine invades history through faith in Christ and liturgical celebration be consistent with his understanding of the eschatological abolition of history through Christ? Eliade's discussion of the regenerative scenarios in *Cosmos and History* gives a hint that the resolution of the conflict might lie in the conceptual situation of the prophets and the early Christians. Incorporating the traditional vocabulary of the periodic regeneration of the world, they spoke of the eternal presence of the transforming events of God by focusing on the contemporary regeneration of the individual. Thus they preserved the tension between present and future. By mixing prophetic and traditional terminology, the Christian vocabulary embraced the individual's transformation as both a present and eventual final deliverance.

> In these spacious Messianic visions it is also easy to discern the very old scenarios of annual regeneration of the cosmos by the repetition of the Creation and by the deliverance of the suffering king. . . . The only difference is that this victory over the forces of darkness and chaos no longer occurs regularly every year, but is projected into a future Messianic *illud tempus.*[42]

The apparent problem is accessible through a limited practice of Eliade's method of metapsychoanalysis on the ideological richness of early Christian language. Eliade thus recognizes that the apparent inconsistency of the Christian terminology is actually an expression of its remarkable and fruitful complexity. The richness of the Christian vocabulary increases as the view that salvation is by the cross is worked out through the existing images of the cosmic tree. As Eliade says, "the salvation revealed by the cross does not annul the pre-Christian values of the tree of the world . . . on the contrary, the cross comes to complete all its earlier valences and meanings. . . ."[43] It is further enriched as elements of initiatory symbolism are worked into the sacraments and the theology of the death and resurrection of Christ. Seen as an irreversible event rather than as an annual occurrence, as in the resurrection of Adonis, the resurrection of Christ symbolized the inbreaking of real time, the eschaton. Eliade goes on to chart the eventual flow of the initiatory symbol, as it carries Christian theology into European literature and the unconscious memories of secular, post-Enlightenment society.[44]

The basic principle in Eliade's thesis of the uniqueness of Christianity is drawn from his view that ritual brings the primordial period into contemporary life. In this case, the life, death, and resurrection of Christ as the exemplary events are reactualized. The Christian escapes from profane time's terrible threat by embracing the reality of the sacred time of Christ.[45] Thus, for Eliade, the demythologization of Bultmann and others is beside the point. The real question about Christianity is whether or not it maintains a "spiritual horizon" and, in light of the secularization of society, the question now becomes whether Christianity can stimulate a recovery of this horizon. Eliade hopes that he will at least help contemporary man to recognize the language of the sacred. By calling attention to the primitive myths and symbols he believes that he will provide a perspective from which we can identify the presence of the sacred in the mythological structures of our own lives. Eliade proposes nothing less than a resacralization and remythologization of the secularized myths of contemporary culture. He is convinced that even with their current distortions, the original mythic patterns retain power for the imagination and can be brought back to life. "The archetype is still creative even though sunk to lower and lower levels."[46]

IV

From this perspective of archaic mythologies, where does Eliade identify the presence of myths in our culture? The obvious public myths include those of

Communism, National Socialism, racism, etc. More subtle and, perhaps in the final analysis, more interesting ones include our fantasies, longings, dreams, and festivities.

Eliade looks at society in the light of the profound mythic theme of the return to the exemplary time, and discovers that education itself fills this function. European education since Livy and Plutarch, and again since the Renaissance, looked to the archetypal virtues and personages of antiquity as models. Hero imitation still remains a fundamental motivation of contemporary education. In addition to education, mythological thinking appears predominantly in our attitude toward time. The popularity of both visual entertainment and reading lies in their capacity for concentrating and heightening the intensity of experienced time. They become substitutes for the magico-religious time of archaic cultures, for they deliver us from our time to different histories and different temporal rhythms. This function of mythological thinking in distractions and amusements is a distinctive characteristic of contemporary life. For "in all traditional societies, every responsible action reproduced its mythical, transhuman model, and consequently took place in sacred time. Labor, handicrafts, war, and love were all sacraments. . . . The true 'fall unto time' begins with the secularization of work."[47]

Eliade's fascination with psychological motifs has led him to write that "it is depth psychology that has revealed the most *terrae ignotae*."[48] Eliade has recognized in Jung's conceptions of the archetypes a realm as primordial as that of the mythological figures of the primitives. Jung's theory suggests to Eliade that a new understanding of religious experience may be in store for Western man. He is in fact closer to mythological realities psychologically than he realizes. This is particularly interesting in respect to the practice of psychoanalysis.

Psychoanalysis can be seen in this context as a contemporary return to the primal time. Within the changed perspectives on history produced by the Jewish and Christian feeling for historical, irreversible time and by the positiveness of secularized Christianity, the primordial is changed into the individual's own childhood. The traumas of one's earliest period are thus envisioned as the critical events which determined the pattern of one's life. Eliade sees the psychoanalytic return to this time of childhood trauma as similar to the primitive's ritual return. In this process the patient reenacts and relives these crises. He brings them to consciousness and contemporizes the creative or destructive epoch.

> We might translate the operative procedure into terms of archaic thought, by saying that the cure is to begin living all over again; that is, to repeat the birth, to make oneself contemporary with 'the beginning' and this is no less than an invitation of the supreme beginning, the cosmogony . . . for the modern man, personal experience that is 'primordial' can be no other than that of infancy. When the psyche comes to a crisis, it is to infancy that he must return in order to re-live and confront anew, the event from which the crisis originated."[49]

While Eliade considers the role of crises and traumas in forming the unconscious, he also recognizes that there are profound harmonies among mental experiences. Subconscious fantasies, psychopathic conditions, conscious activities, and reasoned philosophical views all seem to harmonize with myths. Eliade has thus coined the term, "transconscious," to represent the comprehensive mental faculty, and the phrase, "transconscious logic," to refer to the morphology of its functions.[50]

As we have noted, Eliade believes that myth is a distinct language in itself. We may be tempted to transform myths into other, more secular forms of thought. But would this work out well? Eliade does not believe that the reduction of mythology to profane vocabulary offers a workable solution. Such a reduction, which is illustrated by the demythologization of Bultmann, is seen by Eliade as a disturbing asceticism. It is a denial by Western, European man of his own psychic depths. This is a part of the radical destruction of the language of the arts which characterizes the contemporary artistic mood. It is a "reversion to chaos" in search of a germinal point from which a cultural re-creation may be developed.[51] While Bultmann has determined that existentialist categories are the means for understanding myths today,[52] Eliade has pointed out that comparative mythology provides a way for understanding myths in their own terms. In fact, he believes that comparative mythology provides a way for even analyzing existentialism. Eliade's own appropriation of abstract concepts such as "time," "space," "openness," and "archetype" in his discussion of myth causes us to wonder about the viability of this method. It raises the question of Eliade's success in remaining within the limits he sometimes suggests. Larry G. Shiner has observed:

> Although Eliade's concern with sacred and profane space is a concern with experience not conceptually [sic], his own presentation is, of course, conceptual. In keeping with his polar understanding of sacred and profane, he describes the contrasting spatial experiences of homo religiosus and modern profane man in terms of a series of opposites: homogeneity/heterogeneity, quantity/quality, chaos/cosmos, relativity/absoluteness.[53]

How far, we may ask, can Eliade go in using such concepts before subtly distorting the myths from their *sui generis* meaning? More fundamentally, has Eliade's concept of the "sacred" the same reductive weakness as Bultmann's use of the existentialist category of "decision"? The power of the former concept may well lie in the early experience Eliade had in the worship services of the Eastern Christian tradition in Rumania, as the roots of the concept of Being itself in Tillich's thinking drew from Lutheran services of his own childhood.[54] Questions as to the source of the concept of the "sacred" aside, does it serve to convey the authentic experience of the divine in multiple cults and traditions? Or, on the other hand, does its use tend to obscure important distinctions? In his appreciative essay, Gunter Spältmann, for one, holds that Eliade has indeed found a common denominator in all religious phenomena in the atmosphere of the mysterious, in the feeling that everything is pointing beyond itself to something which will transform the world.[55]

These fundamental questions aside, the possibility remains that Eliade's "spiritual" practice of metapsychoanalysis offers a way around the problems in Bultmann's demythologization. In an article entitled "Where Has Bultmann *Really* Left Us?," Charles E. Carlston criticizes Bultmann's concept of the "Word" as an abstraction.[56] It has become so lean in Bultmann's usage that its meaning is not clear. In contrast, by the retention of the force of mythological language, Eliade offers food to the imagination. In fact, Eliade's attempts to draw his own religious concepts from a phenomenological survey of hierophanies and from myths themselves may enable him to skirt such problems. One of Eliade's most promising contributions at this point lies in his recognition that through myths the sacred deeply touches the whole person. In this respect he is concerned with the mental structure and whole experience of the person who both produces and receives myths. He attempts a description of this structure as the "transconscious" and he proposes that "metapsychoanalysis" gives access to the spiritual experience of the whole person. Tillich also recognized the necessity of a theological comprehension of the psychic processes and his use of philosophical concepts such as being, anxiety, autonomy, heteronomy, etc. were directed toward this end.

Bultmann's consideration of the proclamation of Jesus Christ as the only authentic language-event to which man is called to respond in faith is the second problem mentioned by Carlston.[57] This well known formula of Bultmann is vulnerable because there is no objective criterion for the authentic proclamation. Altizer's criticism of Eliade as inconsistent seems to be appropriate if directed against Bultmann. Does it help us to speak of the distinctive proclamation of Christ if this proclamation seems to be an annihilation of reasoned reflection on Christ? Altizer's rebuttal that the Christian faith must now be described as an accessible possibility is not unjustified. Has Eliade's metapsychoanalysis, which uncovers the religious heterogeneity in these roots of Jewish and Christian traditions, offered a way beyond this problem? In short, do his concerns with ritual re-enactment of the events of Jesus and his recognition of the fibers of cyclic renewal help us to appreciate the richness of the fabric of the early Christian theology? Does understanding the intellectual creativity of the prophets and the apostolic fathers add supportive dimensions of appreciation and loyalty to the act of faith? Has Eliade also given us the game plan for an end run around Anselm's *credo ut intellegam*? This much can be said in answer to these questions. Among philosophers, theologians, historians, etc., there is a growing consensus that recognition of the mythological richness of scientific and historical theories leads to a more open stance and a more understanding commitment.[58] It is worth recalling that when Plato came to the most difficult questions he began to retell the myths.

Considered in the context of epistemological inquiry, Eliade proposes that we admit that we approach reality with the internal categories of myth and archetype. They are the form in which the mind invariably knows reality at its richest; they are the inescapable neo-Kantian categories of perception. Could this mean that Eliade contributes to another Copernican revolution in religious knowledge? Do myths really become the means for awakening secular man to the presence of the sacred, to the conviction that, as Abraham Heschel put it, man is not alone?

Eliade poses an enduring question for us in such a pronounced form that we cannot escape it. In an age in which people are becoming consciously critical of traditional myths, is it possible to escape by faith from the deterioration of historical time? Does the awareness of the escape from historical time inevitably historicize the process?[59] The solution to this insistent question may lie in our facility for recognizing the myths in our own secular lives and following their lead into the traditional wisdom. Eliade believes that this recovery of the sense of the sacred lies in our analysis of the conjunction and interplay of contemporary mythic experience and traditional myths and symbols. This complex of perceptions involves both a close listening to ourselves and a critical awareness of the artistry of myth. It involves the process of metapsychoanalysis. Closely related to this issue is a speculative question concerning the nature of faith. Is the faith of the Christian tradition expressed productively and accurately in the new piety of metapsychoanalysis?

In the final analysis, Eliade leaves us with the enigma of his own method. Is it empirical, phenomenological, or intuitive? While Dorothy Lubby criticizes his work from an anthropologist's concern for an empirical methodology, William Lewa describes his approach as genuinely phenomenological.[60] Whatever else it is, Eliade's method does involve an intuitive sensitivity which enables him to find the configurations of his theory in diverse periods and cultures. This method may, however, involve more of an act of personal faith than Eliade has yet to explore. The mind that perceives the transformation of history in the Incarnation may also be the mind of one who has made an earlier commitment in faith. This eclecticism, however, may in some ways weaken the student's perception of the distinctions among religious traditions. For instance, the significance of the covenant in Israel's theological traditions may be overlooked under the shadow of the concern for universal myths. The clue to Eliade's method may lie, however, despite the complexity of the subject matter and the problems, in a journal entry which he wrote years ago. "My essential preoccupation is precisely the means of escaping history, of saving myself through symbol, myth, rites, and archetypes."[61] With this elegant and deceptively simple statement, many of us have increasing sympathy.

NOTES

[1]Mircea Eliade, *Myth and Reality*, trans. from the French by Willard R. Trask (New York: Harper & Row, 1963), p. 114.

[2]Mircea Eliade, *Birth and Rebirth: The Religious Meaning of Initiation in Human Culture*, trans. from the French by Willard R. Trask (New York: Harper and Brothers, 1958), p. ix.

[3]Mircea Eliade, *Images and Symbols: Studies in Religious Symbolism*, trans. from the French by Philip Mairet (New York: Sheed and Ward, 1969), p. 18.

[4]R. D. Baird, "Normative Elements in Eliade's Phenomenology of Symbolism," *Union Seminary Quarterly Review*, 25 (1970): 507.

[5]Mircea Eliade, *Patterns in Comparative Religion*, trans. from the French by Rosemary Sheed (New York: Sheed and Ward, 1958), p. 426.

[6]Eliade, *Patterns*, p. 426.

[7]Mircea Eliade, *Myths, Dreams, and Mysteries: The Encounter Between Contemporary Faiths and Archaic Realities*, trans. from the French by Philip Mairet (New York: Harper & Row, 1967), pp. 5, 14. (First English edition 1960 by Harvill Press).

[8]Eliade, *Patterns in Comparative Religion*, p. 430.

[9]Eliade, *Myth and Reality*, p. 19.

[10]Eliade, *Myths*, p. 17.

[11]Eliade, *Myths*, p. 18.

[12]Eliade, *Patterns in Comparative Religion*, p. 430.

[13]Robert Leeyster, "Study of Myth: Two Approaches," *Journal of Bible and Religion*, 33 (1966): 235.

[14]Eliade, *Images and Symbols*, pp. 12, 174ff.

[15]Eliade, *Images and Symbols*, pp. 15, 37. See also *Patterns*, p. 428.

[16]Eliade, *Images and Symbols*, p. 121.

[17]M. L. Ricketts, "Nature and Extent of Eliade's Jungianism," *Union Seminary Quarterly Review*, 25 (1970): 221.

[18]Eliade, *Patterns*, p. 433.

[19]John B. Cobb, "Christianity and Myth," *The Journal of Bible and Religion*, XXXIII (1965): 315.

[20]Mircea Eliade, *The Two and the One*, trans. from the French by J. M. Cohen (London: Harvell Press, Ltd., 1965), p. 197.

[21]Eliade, *The Two and the One*, p. 201.

[22]Eliade, *Images and Symbols*, p. 35.

[23]Mircea Eliade, "History of Religions and a New Humanism," *History of Religions*, I (1961): 1-8.

[24]Eliade, *Myths*, p. 16.

[25]Mircea Eliade, *The Sacred and the Profane: The Nature of Religion*, trans. from the French by William R. Trask (New York: Harcourt, Brace and World, Inc., 1959), p. 45.

[26]Eliade, *Myth and Reality*, pp. 24ff., 42.

[27]Eliade, *Birth and Rebirth*, p. xii.

[28]Eliade, *Images and Symbols*, p. 54. See also *Patterns*, pp. 375, 437; *Myths*, pp. 151ff.

[29]Eliade, *Birth and Rebirth*, p. 3.

[30]Eliade, *Myths*, p. 200. See *Birth and Rebirth*, p. xiv.

[31]Mircea Eliade, *Yoga: Immortality and Freedom*, trans. from the French by William R. Trask (New York: Pantheon Books, Inc., 1958), pp. 362ff. See also *Myths*, pp. 90ff.; *The Sacred and the Profane*, pp. 184ff.

[32]Eliade, *Myths*, p. 224.

[33]Eliade, *Birth and Rebirth*, p. 105; *Images and Symbols*, pp. 165ff.

[34]Eliade, *Myths*, p. 183.

[35]See Eliade's six points summarizing the meaning of symbols in *The Two and the One*, pp. 201ff.

[36]Eliade, *Myth and Reality*, pp. 95ff. See also *Patterns*, pp. 46ff., 64ff.

[37]Eliade, *Myth and Reality*, p. 98.

[38]Eliade, *Myths*, pp. 143ff.

[39]Eliade, *Myths*, p. 154.

[40]Mircea Eliade, *Cosmos and History: The Myth of the Eternal Return*, trans. from the French by Willard R. Trask (New York: Harper and Brothers, 1959), pp. 108, 110.

[41]Thomas J. J. Altizer, *Mircea Eliade and the Dialectic of the Sacred* (Philadelphia: The Westminster Press, 1963), pp. 64ff.

[42]Eliade, *Cosmos and History*, p. 105.

[43]Eliade, *Images and Symbols*, p. 164.

[44]Eliade, *Birth and Rebirth*, pp. 118, 122ff.

[45]Eliade, *Myths*, p. 37.

[46]Eliade, *Patterns*, p. 432.

[47]Eliade, *Myths*, p. 37.

[48]Eliade, *The Two and the One*, pp. 9-10.

[49]Eliade, *Myths*, p. 54.

[50]See Eliade, *Patterns*, pp. 450, 454; *Images and Symbols*, pp. 37, 120; Ricketts, *loc. cit.*

[51]Eliade, *Myth and Reality*, pp. 72ff.

[52]Rudolph Bultmann, "New Testament and Mythology," in *Kerygma and Myth*, ed. Hans Werner Bartsch, trans. Reginald H. Fuller (New York: Harper and Brothers, 1961); and in the same volume "Bultmann Replies to his Critics," pp. 191ff. See also Rudolph Bultmann and Karl Jaspers, *Myth and Christianity*, trans. Norman Guterman (New York: The Noonday Press, 1958), pp. 210ff.

[53]Larry E. Shiner, "Sacred Space, Profane Space, Human Space," *Journal of the American Academy of Religion*, XL (1972): 462.

[54]Paul Tillich, *On the Boundary: An Autobiographical Sketch* (New York: Charles Scribner's Sons, 1966). See also Mircea Eliade, "Paul Tillich and the History of Religions," in *The Future of Religions*, ed. Jerald Brauer (New York: Harper & Row, 1966), pp. 31ff.

[55]Gunter Spältmann, "Authenticity and the Experience of Time: Remarks on Mircea Eliade's Literary Works," *Myths and Symbols: Studies in Honor of Mircea Eliade*, eds. Joseph M. Kitagawa and Charles H. Long (Chicago: The University of Chicago Press, 1969), p. 369.

[56]Charles E. Carlston, "Where Has Bultmann Really Left Us?" *Andover Newton Quarterly*, 13 (1972):156-57.

[57]See Rudolph Bultmann, *Jesus Christ and Mythology* (London: SCM Press, Ltd., 1960), p. 84; "New Testament and Mythology," pp. 41-42.; *Existence and Faith*, trans. Schubert M. Ogden (London: Collins, 1960), pp. 107ff.

[58]Langdon Gilkey, *Naming the Whirlwind: The Renewal of God-Language* (Indianapolis: Bobbs-Merrill, 1969); Thomas S. Kuhn, *The Structure of Scientific Revolutions* (Chicago: The University of Chicago Press, 1962); Stephen Toulmin, *Foresight and Understanding* (New York: Harper and Row, 1963).

[59]See Schubert Ogden, *Christ Without Myth* (London: Collins, 1962) for similar critiques of Bultmann's failure to demythologize the kerygma.

[60]Dorothy Lubby, "Review of Birth and Rebirth," *American Anthropologist*, LXI (1959): 240. See the defense of Eliade's methods by William Lewa in his review of *The Sacred and the Profane* in the same issue, p. 242.

[61]Quoted by Virgil Zerunea in his "The Literary Work of Mircea Eliade," in *Myths and Symbols: Studies in Honor of Mircea Eliade*, p. 351.

History as Narrative:
Remembering Creatively

JAMES WIGGINS

FOR the initial meeting of the Myth Seminar of the American Academy of Religion the overreaching concern seemed to be a desire to discover or rediscover the possibility of myth in our time. Lee Gibbs sounded the note on a very personal level: "I am seeking to fill a spiritual vacuum by searching for a renewed sense of the meaning and power of myth."[1] In this sentiment he comes very close to Eric Neumann's observation that: "The malaise of culture is in reality the malaise of life in a world bereft of myth."[2] Such a diagnosis and such a personal quest are to be found in the writings of many others as well. Although the sentiments are widespread among the writings of scholars from a variety of disciplines, such spokesmen typically are explicitly or implicitly scholars profoundly interested in religion, but religion in a world *post mortem dei*. Those who uncritically and simplistically propose some strategy of regression, i.e., of willfully returning to a time when myths were alive and well, bodied forth by a culture sustained by them, can be dismissed. But when sensitivity is expressed toward the impossibility of returning to pre-critical times, and when the goal is expressed as a desire for second naïveté, à la Ricouer, then the thoughtfulness of such thinkers can be taken seriously and their thought engaged at a significant level. Happily, this seminar began with that degree of sophistication.

From the texts of Gibbs' and Weckman's essays and from my memory of Stevenson's essay (enhanced by reference to his book) I discern three strategies to have been at work. Gibbs seems to me to concur largely with the analysis of Eliade,[3] *viz*, (1) that myth and history are clearly to be distinguished; (2) that historians are to be left to their own work and in a sense their contributions are to be celebrated even though the results of critical history sometimes leave one feeling vertigo in the experience of historical relativity; and (3) Christianity as the religion in which Gibbs has great personal interest, is to be reappropriated, if at all, by carefully rediscovering its mythic dimensions, which dimensions are impervious to the historian's criticism. Stevenson is engaged in a task of attempting to call historians' attention to the mythological basis and functions of historiography, even when historians think they are freeing us from myth. Finally, Weckman in his concentration upon myth as narrative raises important questions regarding a number of aspects of the study and understanding of myth, but it seems that his emphasis upon the structural function of myth is the connecting thesis of his essay. These are disparate concerns and seem to suggest the absence of a center which I experienced in the meetings of the seminar in Chicago last year.

On the other hand, this diversity underscores the immensity of the subject and the necessity to limit attention to one aspect or another at any given time. My hope is that we do not, however, imagine it to be our task neatly to divide the subject into its presumed constitutive aspects and treat them *seriatim*.

The interest which informs this essay in fact makes contact with the three approaches cited above and underscores my hope for these explorations proceeding incrementally, regardless of the specificity of topic from author to author. My concern is to suggest that history and myth, though distinguishable (to that extent I agree with Gibbs), are nonetheless very much connected with each other (and therein I have sympathy with Stevenson), albeit not in some fashion that will be satisfied by asserting their functional identity. Further, I am deeply convinced that history is inescapably narrative[4] in form and that the consequences entailed by that are far-reaching.

I. A GLANCE AT THE HISTORY OF HISTORY

It is common among historians of history to trace its rise to the Greeks, particularly to Thucydides and Herodotus, and later to Polybius as one who became more sophisticated in his methodological self-consciousness.

But occasionally one finds a noted historian such as Page Smith giving the laurels to the Hebrews rather than the Greeks. Supporting arguments on both sides are revealing, not in order to decide the question of who really initiated historical thinking so much as better to understand some of the more important differences between the Greeks and the Hebrews.

For the Greeks it is clear that *mythos* was a word designating traditional versions of the past, whereas *historia* denoted an accurate account of the past. What the word *mythos* implies is an uncritical, or better pre-critical, attitude toward the past, temporality, epistemology, etc.; in the case of *historia*, the very word was understood to be built upon *inquiry* to certify an accurate account. This, of course, implies a rising sense of criticality and the emergence of critical objectivity.[5]

On the other hand, according to Page Smith:

> With the Hebrews history transcended chronology for the first time; . . . the Hebrews invented, so to speak, two familiar aspects of history as we think of it today. First, a fulness of characterization (both of individuals and events), the good with the bad, the favorable with the unfavorable; and then the account of a people as a mystical entity. . . . Finally, the Hebrews endowed their history with a meaning, a purpose, and a direction.[6]

Such disputation, regardless of how it is adjudicated, begs many more important questions than may at first be apparent. It is clear, for example, in the cases of both the Greeks and the Hebrews that history, as well as myth, is always narrative in form. It may then be much more fruitful to inquire into the origin and function of storytelling which is the mode of narrative thinking's expression.

II. HISTORY AND NARRATIVE

It would be folly, however, to mean by inquiring after the origin of storytelling an attempt to fix some chronological accuracy regarding when it first occurred.

Rather, I mean to ask about the originating impulse which gives rise in consciousness to telling stories. James Hillman has cogently, and persuasively, observed that "History may be taken as one of the ways the soul muses, one of the ways in which it psychologically reflects life."[7] He continues: "For us history is a psychological field in which fundamental patterns of the psyche stand out; history reveals the fantasies of the makers of history, and at their back and within the fantasies and patterns are the archetypes."[8] Since the reference to "archetypes" in the preceding quotation may be taken to refer to those experienced realities from which myth also arises, then implicitly Hillman is strongly suggesting an originating connection between myth and history. To date much of the exploration of myth and history, especially in efforts at differentiating them, and, more rarely, in attempts at bridging their differences, has proceeded on an exterior plane. What Hillman challenges us to explore is both myth and history in their psychological dimensions. In this challenge he agrees with Vico's dictum, to which Taylor Stevenson has given great attention, that "the true and the made are convertible." Both myth and history can be seen to be both true and made. What differentiates them are the fantasies which they respectively express. In both cases, however, their spontaneous form of expression is narrative. And that can be very deceptive; so deceptive, in fact, that the formal similarity could obscure the distinctions between them.

Although he was scarcely an intentional friend of myth, Aristotle is often cited as having made some important comments on history. In the *Poetics* Aristotle wrote: "The poet and the historian differ not by writing in verse or in prose . . . The true difference is that one [history] relates what has happened, the other what may happen. . . . poetry tends to express the universal, history the particular."[9] The degree to which von Ranke's motto for the historian, *wie es eigentlich gewesen* (as it really was), has remained the hallmark of *Historismus* is eloquent testimony to Aristotle's continued influence right up to the present. Such characterizations of history, however, have been perpetuated primarily, if not exclusively, on the basis of the manifest content of historical accounts. Further, so many of the philosophers of history and the occasional philosophically sensitive historians have concentrated to a very great extent upon the *how* of historiography — the authentication of data, the drawing of inferences, the criteria to be used in assessing historical accounts, the relation of history to other disciplines, especially the social sciences in recent times. Such examinations have frequently subjected historians to being weighed and found wanting by their scientifically minded colleagues. The resultant sense of inferiority contributed mightily to the idolatry of facts in some cases and to the abandonment of the soul of history to the methods of social science in other cases.

But men of insight, sensibility and courage have not been lacking in the historical profession. There have been, even if a minority, those who have kept alive the awareness of narrative as the heart of history. One thinks of Trevelyan writing already in 1913: "history is, in its unchangeable essence, 'a tale.' . . . the art of history remains always the art of narrative."[10] And so the lucid expositions of the contemporary historian, H. Stuart Hughes: "historical prose has always consisted primarily of narrative. Whether we try to bring history closer to social science or to give greater scope to the wanderings of its artistic fancy. . . . The main business, we are reminded, is narrative. . . . As its very name keeps recalling to our minds, history is story."[11] Finally, an exemplary philosopher of history plumbs the point:

> I find it astonishing that no critical philosopher of history has yet offered us a clear account of what it is to follow or to construct an historical narrative. And yet such an account is *plainly essential* to any successful answers to more complicated questions regarding either the nature or the vindication of *historical thinking*.[12]

III. Reimagining Psycho-History

One of the most recent developments in historiography relating to this problem has been the rise of what is being called "psycho-history." Although the courtship is very tentative to date, some important issues are already to the fore. William L. Langer gave official sanction to the courtship in "The Next Assignment," his presidential address to the American Historical Association in 1957, wherein he called upon historians to be more aware of the potential in conjoining psychoanalysis and historiography. Since then Bruce Mazlish, Hans Meyerhoff, Erik Erikson, Robert J. Lifton, Norman O. Brown, *et al.*, have demonstrated in various ways how fruitful a wedding may be. H. Stuart Hughes has distilled from the conversation the following:

> [Psychoanalysis] has shown us that we historians have been right all along in stressing individuality and the unique quality of personal experience. . . . The individual consciousness is our final datum, the bedrock of what we know. . . . Both [psychoanalysis and history] believe in the radical subjectivity of human understanding. . . . Both yearn to escape from the . . . double confinement of the investigator's mind and of that other mind (whether of the historical actor or analysand) with which he is trying to bring his own consciousness into sympathetic response.[13]

In both processes, psychoanalysis and historical accounting, the primary data are those experience expressions which are constitutive of life stories. When the historian writes, a narrative emerges; when the psychoanalytic process is terminated there remains a case history, i.e., a narrative of the process. What we need to explore, then, is what sort of understanding emerges through prose which is primarily narrative and what processes in thinking give rise to narrative.

Memory is the crux of the matter, I believe. History is sometimes described as an attempt at giving expression to a composite memory, i.e., a transcending of the limitations of discreet memories as preserved in documents which provide accounts of the event or period under consideration by cross reference to other such documentary memory deposits. But the assumptions regarding memory in such reports are often naïve in the extreme. The workings of memory have been partially exposed better by the psychoanalytical process. Hillman puts it succinctly:

> Freud began his talking cure by asking patients to follow one basic rule: to let their souls speak without inhibition. . . . When they thus abandoned voluntary control of the intelligibility of understanding, their association led them into *memoria*. Analysis begins with memory and its expression in speech.[14]

Beginning in this way, Freud made a momentous discovery.

> Memory seemed plainly to be a repository of past events — . . . but on closer scrutiny these events turned out to be not actualities but fantasies. In the world they had not happened at all, yet they happened in the memory. Memory, . . . was not only a storehouse of what had happened. It also had a fantasy aspect that affected present and future. To things that had never existed and events that had never happened, memory could give the quality of remembrance, the feeling that they had existed, had happened. Thus memory was truly not bound by time or place. . . . [15]

Historians, however, are similar to Freud in their suspicion of such a view of memory. Nor will invoking the texts of Plato in the *Meno* dialogue or Augustine in his *Confessions* likely appease the suspicions. For modern historians have methodologically supposed it to be the case that they should and could bring memory under rational and volitional control. Historians are often applauded for the degree to which they "have command" of their data. Patients in analysis are often criticized and categorized as neurotic when they apparently do not have their memories under control. But, of course, willing the memory to be purged does not make it so. And historians, similar to patients in analysis, are unable — thank goodness — to prevent the flashes of intuitive insight welling up from *memoria* from enlivening their narrative accounts. Of course historians "re-member" more than the so-called "objective data" will support in their narrative accounts. For, as John Lukacs happily puts the point, the memory is not a camera, it is a darkroom.

Hillman writes that "*Memoria* has the reality of a fundamental power of the soul. It needs no empirical proof."[16] But this observation, which Plato and Augustine would have regarded as self-evident, was very recently lost sight of. In the nineteenth century, Hillman asserts, "we lost our imaginal ego, the ego which speaks for this aspect of the soul [*memoria*]. Instead, we identified wholly with the rational, volitional ego. *Memoria* became unconscious."[17] The implication is clear for modern historiography. The empirically verifiable memory traces — data of whatever sort — to which historians typically give greatest credence are but the expressions of a radically truncated memory and leave much of what matters most in human experience unexplored, and even such as do surface are frequently treated as evidence of neuroses, rather than sources of insight. History, like many forms of psychoanalysis, is in danger of losing soul for want of an adequate acknowledgment of and openness to *memoria*. The saving vestige, however, may lie in the narrative form in which history finds expression.

Why? Narrative implicitly aims at wholeness. This wholistic impulse could never be fulfilled in quantitative terms, i.e., by assembling every last datum which could conceivably be relevant to account for any particular event or series of events. Rather, its wholistic impulse is in the rich overdetermination of its language, which narrative not only permits but evokes from a storyteller. It is not simply that they tell stories that potentially gives import to historians, but rather it is how they tell them. And the "how" is not primarily a matter of rhetorical technique, regardless of the importance of technique. Rather it is a question of the openness of the historian to *memoria*, the basis of which is imagination. Indeed when imagination is given its due, the question of *how* a story is told is superseded. It becomes rather a question of "where," where one imaginatively places one's images and symbolic utterances. In which configuration of associations and resonances does one's accounts of events become transformed? It is not even, finally, a question of accuracy with regard to "when" that marks the great historian. The establishment of chronology is preliminary to the deeper responsibilities and opportunities of the historian, just as the "how" is. By giving voice to narrative the historian transcends the "how" of fact gathering and the "when" of establishing chronology and enters into the realm of his proper art. This observation regarding the artistic function of the historian has tended to be underestimated ever since Aristotle contrasted poetry and history. But it must be mentioned at the outset of discussing narrative in relationship to memory and imagination precisely because in a tradition older than Aristotle, Plato had argued in behalf of the divine origin of the soul. If *memoria* and *imaginatio* are seen as proper functions of the soul, then through them men have traffic with the gods inasmuch as soul (*psyche*) is one of them. Such an assertion seems to accord well with the narrative form of myths which are, even in popular views, held to include stories of the doings of the gods. But what, it may be asked, has such an assertion to do with historical narrative?

The clue is to be found in the memory of history's having a muse. The Muses were nine lovely sisters, daughters of Zeus and Mnemosyne, Memory. According to Hesiod's account of the Muses: "They were all of one mind, their hearts are set upon song and their spirit is free from care. He is happy whom the Muses love." All of the nine, as their activities became differentiated, were in the service of one of the *arts*, which, along with dance, epic poetry, love-poetry, lyric poetry, etc., included astronomy *and history*, the Muse of which was Clio. It is recorded by Hesiod that one day the nine Muses appeared to him and they said, "We know how to speak false things that seem true, but we know how, when we will, to utter true things." In the estimate of the Greeks to be touched by the Muses, any or all, was to be counted sacred beyond the attainment of any priest — so highly were the Muses regarded. From what lofty heights have the sights of historical aspiration descended.

This glance at the story of the Muses was a necessary detour before our next step in exploring historical narrative. The appearance of narrative in historical accounts, more and more checkered as they are by all sorts of "authenticating data" ranging from statistical charts, to maps, to demographic tables, is typically regarded as a shift to the mode of interpretive expression. But more than this, narrative is the form and even in some very deep sense the substance in which the historian's presentation is offered and in taking recourse to, or better, in allowing narrative to express itself, the historian remains within his heritage and deserves his birthright — as an artist whose medium is language and whose expression is literature.

Nor is the historian unique in this. The psychologist, who it might be allowed sometimes encounters Psyche in his encounters with people, often begins analysis with the words "Tell me about it." What is required is an ear attuned to hearing one snatch of a patient's memory and then another as all figuring into some story or another. Hillman puts it as having the ears to hear "case material" as a tale.[18] By an almost precise analogy I believe that historians must have sensibilities so attuned as to be able to hear and envision the data they collect as a tale or a story.

But such sensibility training is difficult to come by. The strategy proposed by many among the current spate of psycho-history theorists is one which almost invariably turns upon or to Freudian assumptions. But a much more promising direction is to be found in the works of Jung and certain Jungian inspired thinkers such as James Hillman and David L. Miller. In these instances the psyche's inextricable involvement with mythology is presupposed. Thus, historians who have caught a vision of the possibilities inherent in a collusion between psychology and history will do far better to start with a study of Jung's writings rather than Freud's. But my bias needs amplification.

In his autobiography Jung time and again reiterates the importance of "story" to his thought and work. Even though it is the case that *de facto* historians have consistently told stories as their mode of expression, what one detects in many a reflection on historiography, is a sense of inferiority for doing so, often coupled with a longing for some way of being less vulnerable to criticism from their more empirically inclined colleagues in other disciplines. What some depth psychologists have had to fight their way through to, *viz.*, the legitimacy of telling tales as expressions of their creative work, historians have often been embarrassed by. This essay is precisely an expression of the conviction that historians, insofar as they have been the instruments of narrative expression, should celebrate that and imaginatively reflect upon the inherent opportunity presented by this narrative heritage.

Mircea Eliade has given currency to the phrase "the terror of history" in his rigorous distinction between myth and history (cf. *Cosmos & History*). His position presupposes that the fall into historical consciousness out of mythic modes of perception inevitably leads to the impasse of experiencing events in time as meaningless. The one safeguard he offers is his conviction that

> it is only by presupposing the existence of God that he [the modern man and/or the Christian] conquers, on the one hand, freedom (which grants him autonomy in a universe governed by laws . . .) and, on the other hand, the certainty that historical tragedies have a transhistorical meaning, even if that meaning is not always visible for humanity in its present condition. Any other situation of modern man leads, in the end, to despair.[19]

This view is predicated upon his view that modern man has abandoned "the paradise of archetypes and repetitions."[20] The thrust of my insistence upon the importance of narrative in the thought of the historian, not to mention other groups of major practitioners of narrative, the novelists, now being augmented by certain depth psychologists, indicates that it may be a premature judgment to hold that modern man has abandoned mythic consciousness.

In fact, Eliade has himself noted that many people today, though chronologically living in modernity, have hardly abandoned modes of mythic consciousness. Such an observation underscores a recurrent historiographical problem, *viz.*, that chronology and psychology are by no means identical, thus such assertions as "they were 'throw-backs,' " and "he was ahead of his time." But even more to the point, in a little noticed article published fourteen years after the original appearance of *Le Mythe de l'eternal retour*, Eliade wrote:

> Modern man, fallen under the domination of Time and obsessed by his own historicity, should try to "open himself" to the World by acquiring a new dimension in the limitless realm of Time. Unconsciously he defends himself against the historiographic *anamnesis* that opens perspectives he could not possibly suspect if, following Hegel's example, he had confined himself to "communing with the Universal Spirit" while reading his newspaper every morning. ... This historiographical anamnesis continues the religious valorization of memory and forgetfulness. [21]

Only a few paragraphs prior to the passage just cited Eliade, referring to the rise of so-called "universal history," observed that the "vertiginous widening of the historical horizon" is one of the few encouraging syndromes in the modern world. In his words "But that is not all: through this historiographic *anamnesis* man *enters deep into himself....* A true historiographic *anamnesis* finds expression in the discovery of our solidarity with vanished or peripheral people."[22]

Isaak Dineson's oft-quoted remark that "Any sorrow can be borne if a story can be told about it" can be paraphrased to suggest that any terror history can impose can be borne if a story can be told. The movement will be one, à la Goethe, of turning life into art, and transforming art into life. Historians have the opportunity and obligation to let active imagination loose upon collective *memoria*. Then, trusting the process, it may sometimes happen that the lives of those who hear the historian's tale will be able to bear the terror of history in a fashion which transforms the terror. The promise beckons, as Jung puts it, not that we will see different things, but rather that, in this case through the historian's story, we may see the same things differently.

The reference to active imagination must be underscored. The subtitle of this paper "creatively remembering" is pointing precisely to this. In attempts at narrative which turn out to be failures, one suspects that often the failure lies in a very specific error. It is the failure to recognize the need for imagination in ordering a story. What is substituted for Clio's touch are acts of forced reason or will. The results are often contrivances and cuteness, which pale beside instances of the genuine article. What is lacking is an openness to the richness of *memoria* which provides depth and substance for active imagination. In the writing of history the discipline required is that of constantly guarding against the temptation of treating the datum at hand, whether it be a document, an artifact, a statistical chart, a tombstone epitaph, or whatever, in its literal giveness as if it exhausted that in which the historian is most deeply interested. What one may probe for, alternatively, is the mode of consciousness, i.e., the fantasy which was operating in the agent which expressed itself in such a precise fashion. To write, for example, the history of Christianity, a vexing and taxing undertaking as I can testify to, requires giving attention to a wide variety of resources — ecclesiology, ecclesiastical organization, liturgy, ethics, behavioral patterns, theological treatises, prayer books, etc., almost *ad nauseum*. The temptation to which many who have tried their hand have succumbed is a rational and willful ordering of the data. With very few exceptions such as Charles Williams' *The Descent of the Dove*, yet to be written, to my knowledge, is a truly imaginative history of Christianity. What one finds more examples of, however, are some notable instances of autobiography — one thinks immediately of *The Confessions* — and biography. When and if the imaginative history of Christianity, or any religious tradition, is written, one must suppose that much of the data cited will be the same as in the standard histories. Further, the same passion for precision will be there. What will be qualitatively different, however, I suspect, will be the artful communication of the realization that the author has moved beyond the bondage of literalism. What will be gained in such a narrative for those who still regard themselves as Christian, Buddhist, Muslim, or whatever, will not be freedom from the past in any simplistic fashion, but rather *distance*. Thereby, potentially, a revitalization of what has become literalized and reified may occur, i.e., a connection with what I can only call the archetypal substance of the data (the givens) may be experienced both as true and as made. Concepts may become metaphors; life in the terror of history may be transformed into soul-making. But for that to happen, of course, Clio will have to be erotically cherished, rather than willfully avoided or coerced. And, if it happens, the warfare between myth and history will be itself an unmourned casualty; their complementarity will become more apparent.

NOTES

[1]Lee Gibbs, "Myth and the Mystery of the Future," essay prepared for the Myth Seminar of the American Academy of Religion, 1973.

[2]Eric Neumann, "Die Mythische Welt und der Einzelne," *Eranos Jahrbuch* (Zurich: Rhein-Verlag, AG, 1949), p. 222.

[3]Mircea Eliade, *Cosmos and History: The Myth of the Eternal Return* (New York: Harper Torchbook, 1959), *passim*; and *Myth and Reality* (New York: Harper & Row Publishers, Inc., 1963), *passim.*

[4]In my essay "Story" in Daniel C. Noel, ed.,*Echoes of the Wordless Word* (Missoula, Montana: AAR & SBL, 1973), pp. 175ff., I attempted to explore narrative discourse in some detail. In the context of this essay, "narrative" connotes the sort of imaginative thinking which spontaneously underlies storytelling.

[5]I am not asserting that such aspirations were yet comparable to the Promethean aspiration which has beguiled so many post-Cartesian practitioners of historiography. That fate was not fully visited upon the Greeks in my opinion, although Gilbert Murray's phrase "failure of nerve" in regard to the post-Aristotelean world suggests how near they may have come.

[6]Page Smith, *The Historian and History* (New York: Random House, Inc., 1966), pp. 5-7, *et passim.*

[7]James Hillman, *The Myth of Analysis* (Evanston: Northwestern University Press, 1972), p. 126. Hillman is a Jungian analyst who lives in Zurich. Formerly clinical director of the Jung Institute in Zurich and currently editor of the journal *Spring*, he is an original thinker who defies easy classification. Depth psychology, mythology, history, philosophy and theology have all received creative consideration in his several writings to date.

[8]Hillman, *Myth of Analysis*, pp. 726-27. No less important in this regard is to discover the fantasy of the historiographer.

[9]Aristotle, *Poetics*,trans. S. H. Butcher (New York: Hill & Wang, Inc., 1961), chap. ix, p. 68.

[10]Fritz Stern, ed., *Varieties of History*, Pt. II, 1 "Clio Rediscovered" (New York: World Publishing Co., 1956), p. 236.

[11]H. Stuart Hughes, *History as Art and As Science* (New York: Harper and Row, 1964), pp. 68-69.

[12]W. B. Gaillie, *Philosophy and the Historical Understanding* (New York: Shocken Books, Inc., 1968), p. 9. Italics added.

[13]Hughes, *History as Art*, p. 63, *et passim.*

[14]Hillman, *Myth of Analysis*, p. 169.

[15]Hillman, *Myth of Analysis*, p. 169.

[16]Hillman, *Myth of Analysis*, p. 172.

[17]Hillman, *Myth of Analysis*, p. 173.

[18]Hillman, *Myth of Analysis*, p. 193.

[19]Eliade, *Cosmos and History*, p. 162.

[20]Eliade, *Cosmos and History*, p. 162.

[21]Mircea Eliade, "Mythologies of Memory and Forgetting," *History of Religions*, (Winter 1963): 344.

[22]Eliade, "Mythologies of Memory," 343.

Mythohistory Via Carl Jung:
Where the Historian's Language
is Spoken Without Him

ADELE B. MCCOLLUM

INSTEAD of viewing historiography as the chronicling and interpretation of factual occurrences and events, mythohistory seeks a way of listening to history as the story of events playing out in *maya*. It assumes that history consists, as Alan Watts would say, of stories of God playing hide and seek with himself. This is not to imply that history is either unreal or unnecessary. Just as it is through *maya* that the Real becomes known, so through history can the Real or Being Itself be made known to us. History is therefore necessary. But it is necessary precisely because it is open to symbolic interpretation. When it is no longer consciously symbolic it loses its full potential for carrying us through to a meaningful encounter with Reality.

This essay also makes the assumption that human consciousness is a necessary part of history's full realization of itself. The consciousness of the historian about his task is seen as an integral part in the fulfillment of history. To this end, the historian's consciousness is explored in terms of the four ego functions described by Carl Jung as thinking, feeling, sensation, and intuition.

Thinking and sensation, one must insist, have dominated the awareness of historians in the West since Thucydides. These are the functions which tell us *that* something is and *what* it is. The renascence of myth studies is taken to be indicative of some failure of history for the contemporary situation. Myth, as a spontaneous product of the collective unconscious, may be attempting to make us aware of our condition. This warning is taken into account and the functions most likely to be neglected or subverted in the contemporary consciousness, that is, intuition and feeling, are added to the doing of history. This is done in order to balance the dominant functions of thinking and sensation, and thus to remedy the one-sidedness of history. Because they have been subverted, that is, have been removed from direct conscious control, intuition and feeling allow the contents of the unconscious to filter directly into consciousness without interference from the ego.

Yet another assumption is made here. Out of their ontological unity the Really Real and the collective unconscious resonate with and reflect one another in such a way that one becomes conscious through the other.

It is also asserted that a true symbol potentially allows the whole pleroma to be seen through it. When the collective unconscious can be seen through history-as-symbol by way of the addition of the two subverted functions of feeling and intuition, then Reality becomes available through history in such a way that what is being spoken looks no longer like either myth or like history but like a combination of the two which can be called "myth-history." Mythohistory comes into being by way of mythopoiesis and may be seen as an alternative to the other forms of psychohistory now being written.

All history is psychohistory. Our difficulty is that "We have lost the feel of the fact."[1] While the term "psycho-history" has been appropriated by Freudians and Neo-Freudians working primarily in the area of psychobiography, it is not necessarily exhausted by this particular methodology.[2] The conscious conjoining of psyche or soul with history can as well begin with Jung as with Freud. Jung uses the term "psyche" to connote the totality of all psychic processes, conscious as well as unconscious, and we can, therefore, infer that psycho-history will include both conscious and unconscious elements. In that case, it will also move us beyond the usual linear facticity of current historiography to some other, as yet unknown, dimensions.

Without embarking on a history of historiography one can still claim that the particular brand of scientific historiography emanating from the eighteenth and nineteenth centuries has left us believing that our lived experience is linear, or, if it is not, it should be; and that experience which falls outside the pale of linearity also falls outside the range of normality. This overinflated sense of directed movement through time has led us into a progressivism by means of which we expect a better society if we are oriented toward social transformation, or eschatological fulfillment if we are oriented to the other-worldly. In addition to leaving us with a consciousness of the "forward movingness" of existence, historians, in arrogating to their work the scientific method, have misled us into believing that history deals with "facts" alone in order to arrive at *the* truth.

If the primary value of anything resides in its ability to enrich human experience and understanding, it would seem that we must rethink any methodology or attitude which serves to reduce this experience and understanding to that which can be fully and objectively known. Dream, myth, mystic vision, art, and story all point toward areas of experience that remain partially veiled, and which at the same time remain almost entirely unaccounted for by historicism. That history has not functioned in such a way as to burrow into the depths of human existence became clear to me while teaching a session on myth and history in a religion and culture course. Having established that myth is not a lie, and having discussed its particular value as a means of making a connection with Being Itself, I acknowledged the raised hand of one student who queried: "I don't understand why there have to be all these different stories and interpretations. Surely some historian can look at all of them and tell us which is the right one so we could just learn one." Pure and simple! My student expected the historian to be the one who should narrow down our alternatives so that we need not expose ourselves to the vitality of multifaceted existence.

Despite this discouraging outlook we can, without extensive investigation, regard history as, in part, composed of language. It is the linguistic reiteration of events believed to have occurred, and societies which have not recorded this reiteration in a particular way are said to be non-historical or pre-historic. It is word, used to imitate fixed extraneous forms or events, which defines culture as historical. Word, believed to copy a tangible, objective reality is historical word.

However, language and word have another dimension whose referent is a reality which can never be adequately portrayed. This is the symbolic dimension in which the same language used historically to refer to a given fixed reality now posits a world of its own and conceals as much as it reveals.[3] It is on this symbolic dimension of history that we now need to focus in order to overcome the tendency toward reductionism which occurs when language is used to equate form or event with word. As Progoff says, "There is the special quality of the symbolic process that carries the self-balancing wisdom of life. The inherent capacity of the universe to heal and reintegrate itself in its individual parts is made accessible to man through the symbolic dimension."[4]

Progoff here uses the word "symbol" much the way Jung uses it to refer to our speaking about that which cannot be fully explained. It is necessary to make the distinction between this use of the words, symbol and symbolic, and that of Erich Fromm and many contemporary linguists who would say that all language is symbolic. What Fromm calls a conventional symbol, by means of which a word such as "dog" stands for a conventionally agreed upon object which barks and has four legs, we call a sign and say that such a word has significatory value rather than symbolic value.[5] That which Progoff and Jung call symbolic more closely resembles Fromm's idea of the Universal symbol. The notion that symbol can introduce an awareness of a wisdom of life somehow not available to immediate sensory awareness presupposes, of course, a diabiotic understanding of the world. Through such an understanding it is seen that within, but veiled by, the world of appearances lies a realm of cosmic wisdom, Being Itself, or whatever one wants to call it, which must necessarily be made conscious if human existence is to be made whole. Being is found, then, by making conscious what has been unconscious, and history can be a means of doing precisely that.

If we can come to see the symbolic process at work in history, then history itself comes to have the capacity to expose the "self-balancing wisdom of life." It, too, along with the other human endeavors of myth, literature, the arts, and religions, has power of healing and reintegrating; and history, written historiography, becomes a process of soul-making: psychohistory.

But historians have told us, heretofore, that they deal with what is particular and unique in the course of human events. In fact, that is what they are concerned with: events, as they succeed one another in time. Psyche, on the other hand, connects with the universal, to that which belongs to all of us. Psyche is quite capable of living both in and out of time because she envelops both the realm of linear consciousness and the realm which Jung calls the collective unconscious, that vast wellspring of image in which we all participate.[6] It is psyche who heals and reintegrates and lives apart from time as we usually know it. Ego by itself exists through time as that conscious "I" moving on historically. Psyche goes on, not in sequence, but *in illo tempore*, like myth. But, if we are going to claim a symbolic dimension for history, and to assert that all history is also psychohistory, then it seems we must also find, for history, a way in which it can flow both in and out of time. In order to do this, history as cultural canon, as objective data, as fact, will have to be seen to connect with the same planes of existence occupied by psyche.

What are the grounds for making such a connection between psyche and historiography, and is there any sense in which such an integration can be made without reducing one or the other? Quite obviously it is insufficient to ask, "What is written history symbolic of?" since to name the "what" is to leave us with significatory value but not symbolic value. That is to say that to provide a ready object to complete the equation would be to render it a sign rather than a symbol and would preclude its participating in the realm of Being Itself. Just as the Tao which can be spoken is not the true Tao, the symbol which is fully known is no longer a symbol. By providing the symbol with an objective referent we have made it a closed equation rather than an open potentiality.

Instead of facilely providing this object, we should inquire how a historical fact *feels* and with what in our own lived existence it connects. Efforts to make such inquiries of history must, immediately, seem to herald a kind of presentism. Nonetheless, I should like to deny that this is necessarily the case. Presentism is, itself, another kind of reductionism in that it examines history in order to select those data which seem to have direct relevance or utilitarian value and then disposes of the rest. (The process is similar to Bultmann's method of demythologization which abandons the symbolic in favor of that which can readily be acknowledged as true to contemporary existence. The problem, of course, is both that the seemingly irrelevant historical data and the three-storied universe do have immediate meaning for contemporary existence, and also that we have become so alienated from our psychic life as to be unable to connect with that meaning.) The process I am suggesting, on the other hand, assumes that all historical data are relevant because they are a product of the symbol making function. If we cannot find the connection it is not because the historiography is meaningless but because we are unaware of the scope of our own existence, and are unable to see any connection between our selves and the historiographical word. That is to say, we are often aware *that* something occurred and can frequently define *what* that occurrence was. That it is connected to or has value for our essential being is something which, more often than not, escapes us.

Identifying that which exists and forming conceptual ideas about it would seem to belong primarily to two of the four functions of ego to which Carl Jung refers throughout his work.[7] These four functions, thinking, feeling, sensation and intuition, are all important elements of Jung's work. Because they are functions of ego which refer to the external world, but, at the same time, have peculiarities of development which allow them to relate to the inner unconscious world as well, they may provide an unusually helpful starting point for relating Jung's ideas to the doing of history.

The function which Jung termed "sensation" is similar to that which we might call sense perception. It provides a way of relating to the physical world and it is through this function that we learn *that* something is. Jung identified a second function as "thinking." This has, rightly or wrongly, come to mean what he called directed thinking rather than fantasy thinking, which Jung later referred to as intuitive thinking and which retains a close association with the function of intuition. It is thinking which tells us *what* something is once sensation has established *that* it is.

It appears that the doing of history has been dominated by the two functions of sensation and thinking, the faculties by which we learn of the existence and qualities of a thing. This is hardly surprising since Western scholarship has emphasized the importance of identifying facts and acquiring knowledge of them. This exaggerated stress upon the conceptual and ideational forms of knowing has served to obliterate the scholar's awareness of those two remaining functions which oppose and provide a tension with sensation and thinking, namely, feeling and intuition. The deceptiveness of this one-sided reliance on sensation and thinking has, with but a few exceptions, gone unnoticed, although Jung, himself, gave ample warning of its effects.

> Intellectual understanding and aestheticism both produce the deceptive, treacherous sense of liberation and superiority which is liable to collapse if feeling intervenes. Feeling always binds one to the reality and meaning of symbolic contents . . .[8]
>
> Intuition gives outlook and insight; it revels in the garden of magical possibilities as if they were real.[9]

Here we have, in the two functions of feeling and intuition, the introduction of symbolic possibility and the magical "as if." The sense of the symbolic and the connectedness of intuition have been lacking from Western historiography while it has been devoting itself almost entirely to uncovering obscure data and describing it in such a way as to put it within the grasp of the conceptualizing mind. That is to say, history has been concerned to give knowledge *that* events or persons existed and *what* those events or persons were or did. It has avoided giving attention to its own symbolic meaning and to its own potential for connecting lived reality with observed reality.

Within the framework of Jungian psychology, thinking, feeling, sensation, and intuition are functions of the ego; they either are or can be conscious. However, within the individual there remains a propensity for so overemphasizing one function that one or more of the others is subverted and becomes unconscious. This subverted function is referred to as the inferior function and, due to its subverted condition, can act as a channel through which unconscious contents can filter into ego consciousness. This inferior function should be looked upon as such, more because it is through it that one experiences the underworld of archetypal activity rather than because it is a less important function. Indeed, because it is undeveloped, refers to the unconscious, and cannot be "managed" by the ego, it becomes more important to imaging and symbolizing than the fully developed functions.

In the case of our historians who have overdeveloped the functions of thinking and sensation, the opposing functions of feeling and intuition have become subverted and, for the most part, remain unconscious. Thus, the binding to the reality and meaning of symbolic contents as well as the intrigue of that which is not yet, or the magical "as if," has been eliminated from Western history since, as we see in the above quotations from Jung, these meanings come to us through feeling and intuition.

This does not mean, however, that the reality and meaning of the symbolic and of the "as if" are not present in history and historiography. It simply means that they have disappeared from our immediate perception; history seems to have lost its connection with our lived reality, with the "way things really are."

To insist on the symbolic quality of history is to insist that attention be given to the realms of feeling and intuition; it is to ask that history be written and read through the now inferior functions which are our remaining connections with the unconscious realm of psyche. It is to say that history has, heretofore, made its appeal to consciousness and now to ask that it make its appeal to the deeper levels of soul, to those worlds which remain veiled and unconscious. It is to ask that history be seen as an externalization of the internal, as a symbol system growing out of some lost level of awareness. This, of course, rests on the assumption that what we do and our perceptions of what we have done begin in psychic experience and only then become externalized and objectified. That is to say, history is real insofar as it is first fantasy and then fantasy believed to be fact. This is in no way intended to reduce history to a "nothing but" because, quite clearly, given our present rapture with consciousness, the external is essential to the re-cognition, the knowing again, of the internal. As with the Tao, one and one make One. By reading external historiography as symbol, "as if" its story is the story of our inner worlds, we come to know again, to re-cognize, that which has been lost to us but which is intimately ours. The past then will not be seen as linear past time, but as that which once was but which is still to be lived. In other words, the past is both behind us and ahead of us.

This claim that history is symbolic would seem to place it in the same category with myth, art, dream, and poetry. That is a peculiar claim in this day and age. There is, to be sure, a difference. One feels a difference between a poem read and a history read. Myth, dream, art, and poetry are less veiled, somehow, than history. One views them and knows that they speak from a different place than does history or theology or philosophy. They are not so removed from what lies below the surface. Perhaps this is because they are written or imaged through the functions of feeling and intuition, unlike history which is conceptualized and written through the functions of thinking and sensation. Myth, dream, story, and art filter through the mythopoeic process rather than through the cognitive process. Let us say, then, that art, myth, dream, story, and poetry are primary manifestations of psyche, once removed from the unconscious depths. However, if the functions of feeling and intuition are employed to read theology or history or even political science, the symbolic quality of these may also be perceived. We might call these particular cultural systems secondary manifestations of psyche which result from the dominance of the thinking rational functions being employed in the interpretation of primary manifestations. It may work something, like this: feeling, intuition, and nondirected or intuitive thinking are activated and myth may result. Theology then applies directed thinking to the myth, and doctrine results. In the same way historiography utilizes directed thinking to interpret story and the result is scientific history devoid of soul.

When a primary manifestation is interpreted through another function, one which is in our time less conscious, might we not get something other than positivism? Norman Brown has said that the proper response to poetry is poetry. We may surmise that even a Freudian revisionist would eschew scientific criticism or interpretation of poetry via directed thinking and sensation. If theology were to be interpreted through the functions of feeling and intuition the result might look more like mysticism and might regain the vivid imagery which can appeal to our lived experience. All of this is to inquire whether viewing a secondary manifestation of psyche such as history through an inferior function might return it to a primary manifestation such as art, poetry, dream, or story which can then be read back to psyche.

To view history in this way, as symbol system, is to say that history refers also to things which cannot be established as physical facts. This is not to say that no historical, physical facts exist, but it is to assert that history, if it wishes to be a living vital reality, cannot justify its existence on the basis of its literal verifiability. If it wishes to participate in the symbolic life which is necessary to the unfolding of the cosmic wisdom, to our becoming aware of the pleroma, then it cannot remain literalistic or positivistic. The very act of calling history symbolic places it in the realm of the unknown or incomprehensible as we shall see from Jung's definitions of symbol. Asking a historian to write history which admits a dimension of incomprehensibility and which has its referent in the unknown is undoubtedly some sort of academic heresy. Nevertheless, it seems unlikely that history can offer much understanding of the past or the present, much less claim to be a "field encompassing field," if it gives no credence to one half of human existence, that which is unconscious in our psychic life. It is fortunate for historiography that even when the writer intended to deal only with the facts, the symbolic eye of the reader was not always blinded. This may be because "Whether a thing is a symbol or not depends chiefly on the *attitude* of the observing consciousness; for instance, on whether it regards a given fact not merely as such but also as an expression for something unknown."[10]

If we follow Jung's work on symbol, we find that nearly anything can be symbolic if it is observed with a consciousness which assumes that it implies something more which eludes our immediate knowledge. While Jung realizes that there are, clearly, those things which can hardly be other than symbolic since they would make no sense at all if taken to be literal facts, he also realizes that the eye of the observer is an important factor for what he calls the symbolic attitude. He cites the triangle with an eye within as something manifestly symbolic. He finds that expressions which do not work in such an immediate way to connect us with that which we intuit and feel are either extinct symbols or are products whose symbolic nature depends on the perception of the observing consciousness. Those products which I have called secondary manifestations of psyche, and history in particular, would seem to be expressions whose symbolic nature depends on the beholder. In the work cited above, Jung also recognizes the existence of those who subordinate meaning to the sheer facts. This would seem to be the attitude of many historians, and I would reassert that this particular attitude results from the dominance of the functions of sensation and directed thinking which have been so highly valued in the West.

Jung has yet other qualifications for identifying a living symbol:

> A symbol always presupposes that the chosen expression is the best possible description or formulation of a relatively unknown fact, which is none the less known to exist or is postulated as existing.

> So long as a symbol is a living thing, it is an expression for something that cannot be characterized in any other or better way.

> A symbol really lives only when it is the best and highest expression for something divined but not yet known to the observer. It then compels his unconscious participation and has a life-giving and life-enhancing effect.[11]

I should like to look briefly at historiography in the light of these three quotations. I have placed them in this order not only because they occur so in Jung's text, but also because they seem to provide a gradual elaboration on a single theme.

It is fair to assume that the historian perceives himself to be uncovering some unknown fact which is postulated as existing. This postulation is, in itself, a product of imagination and employs the function of intuition which detects possibilities. I have yet to have a historian tell me that he selected his subject matter by intuition. Most often he cites the fact that the material has not been dealt with previously or its import in affecting the world situation as his reason for choosing this work. Our historian then gathers his data and proceeds to compile it in the best possible description or formulation that he is able. But how does he know this when he has finished gathering his data? And how does he sift through a massive amount of material and select that which is pertinent? He employs the function of feeling to tell him what is of value for his work and what is not. He uses his intuition to inform him that he has compiled sufficient information or that he has done as much as is possible. He has absolutely no way of verifying that there is not more data to be had except by allowing his intuition to tell him that he has collected enough. As Alan Watts once said, it could be decided as well by casting the *I Ching*. When the historian has finished collecting and compiling he finds that his formulation cannot be expressed, at least by him, in any better way.

The analogy between symbol and history would seem to break down when we come to the third quotation, for when the historian is finished he thinks he knows what he has observed even though what he thinks he knows has been informed by the unknown. What was originally divined to be of import he now thinks is known, and most likely our historian would deny any participation of his unconscious; and so, for him, his work is not symbolic but literal. Nevertheless, when this story is read with the symbolic attitude, the historiography remains symbol. When it is not so read it is extinct and calls up no depth of meaning and strikes no resounding chord in psyche.

However, if we assume that the historian is saying more than he intends, it may be that history may still be symbolic even when it is not read with the symbolic attitude. For, "The symbol is always a product of an extremely complex nature, since data *from every psychic function* have gone into its making."[12] This is to say that while the historian may be consciously aware of appealing to the rational functions of thinking and sensation, he remains unaware of the unconscious content which has informed his work through the feeling and intuitive functions. Nevertheless, all four of the Jungian functions have been employed even though the historian is unaware of their activity, and so his work inadvertently is potentially symbolic rather than literal. The possibility that intuition and feeling entered the doing of history, even if the historian refuses to acknowledge their presence, leaves open the alternative of reading history as symbol. The failure of the historian to acknowledge the unconscious psychic element at work in his writing does not mean that he has been able to deny this element in practice. It remains at work whether or not he or his readers choose to admit it. Nonetheless, this prevalent failure to recognize what is going on has left us with a one-sided history which often fails to function as symbol even though the potential for such functioning is inherently there. Consequently, history has become dead, meaningless fact which touches nothing in our spiritual aspirations and evokes none of our vital energies. Neither we nor the historian expect it to do that. History, perceiving itself to be only rational, has robbed itself of its potential as a life-enhancing force among us. It has not lived with the tension of its own non-rational component, and has not felt its own livedness nor intuited its powers for connecting fact with profundity. In contrast, symbolic history occurs when the truly living symbol unites the conscious and unconscious by employing all four functions and allowing unconscious material to enter our awareness through the inferior functions. History, like myth, can tell us "how things really are."

Scientific historicism, of which von Ranke is perhaps the most prominent example, is symptomatic of the state of culture. Jung finds that where there is the subordination of one function the resulting product will be not symbol but symptom, a symptom of the antithetical function which has been repressed.[13] Insofar as history is symptom and not symbol it cannot heal or redeem because it denies to certain psychic activity the right to exist. Assuming that healing, redeeming, making whole, means, at least in part, making available to human awareness all modes and realms of being and meaning, history has failed whenever it has denied its participation in the realm of the sacred, numinous, downward transcendence of psychic life.

I think this failure of history has been sensed by many and is in part responsible for the increased interest in the relationship between myth and history expressed in this seminar. In a time when we are receiving intimations of pluralism, polytheism, and protean man we ought not to disallow any areas of experience to enter our consideration. If returning a symbolic reading to historiography makes available to our understanding areas of reality heretofore ignored or consciously repudiated by that discipline, so much the better. Let history stand alongside of myth as another symbol system in the cultural canon. Psyche will not be permanently denied, and where she has been denied in historiography she has surfaced in myth as a primary manifestation of the unknown. The current interest in the study of mythology can be seen as another indication of the failure of historiography. From the time Thucydides corrected Herodotus, myth and history have become more and more separated with history taking over in the rational realm and myth being repudiated as subjective feeling and intuition. Consequently myth has been seen to lack credibility and history has become so reductive that it cannot admit its symbolic content at all. In order for historiography to come to its full potential as a catalyst of Being alongside of myth, it will need to become mythohistory and admit that it makes use of all four functions, thereby providing a symbol system by means of which we can affirm our hidden sources of remembrance. When it does not do this it cannot offer a wholistic expression of our experience and instead becomes the agent of reductionism as my student wished it to be, or, as my eleven-year-old daughter grumbled into her homework one evening, "I hate history; it says that's all there is."

NOTES

[1]Archibald MacLeish, "To Face the Real Crisis: Man Himself," *New York Times Magazine*, December 25, 1960.

[2]The best known of these psychobiographies include Alexander L. George and Juliette L. George, *Woodrow Wilson and Colonel House*; Erik H. Erikson, *Young Man Luther* and his *Gandhi's Truth*. For a brief review of the literature see Bruce Mazlish, ed., *Psychoanalysis and History* (New York: Grosset and Dunlap, Inc., 1971).

[3]For additional discussion on this matter see Ernst Cassirer, *Language and Myth*, trans. Susanne Langer (New York: Dover Publications, Inc., 1953).

[4]Ira Progoff, "Introduction to the Paperback Edition," *The Symbolic and the Real* (New York: McGraw Hill Book Company, Inc., paperback edition, 1973), p. xiii.

[5]Erich Fromm discusses these uses of the word symbol in *The Forgotten Language* (New York: Grove Press, Inc., 1957), pp. v-23.

[6]Carl Jung's understanding of the collective unconscious is elaborated throughout his works. For a concise description see *Analytical Psychology: Its Theory and Practice* (New York: Vintage, 1970). Jung always finds the collective unconscious to be a universal phenomenon, the contents of which remain unconscious but out of which arise archetypal images which give intimations of the content of the collective unconscious.

[7]See C. G. Jung, "Definitions," *Psychological Types*, trans. R. F. C. Hull, Bollingen Series XX, vol. 6, *The Collected Works of Carl Jung*, (Princeton: Princeton University Press, 1971), pp. 408-86.

[8]C. G. Jung, "The Psychology of the Transferenee," *The Practice of Psychotherapy*, trans. R. F. C. Hull, 2nd ed., Bollingen Series XX, vol. 16, *The Collected Works of Carl Jung*, (Princeton: Princeton University Press, 1966), pp. 279-89.

[9]Jung, "Psychology of the Transference," p. 281.

[10]Jung, *Psychological Types*, p. 475.

[11]Jung, *Psychological Types*, pp. 474-76.

[12]Jung, *Psychological Types*, p. 478. Italics mine.

[13]Jung, *Psychological Types*, pp. 477-80.

Believing Myth as Myth

George Weckman

MYTH is an especially problematic word (like cleave, sanction, and oversight, to name a few), since it not only bears a variety of meanings but even some which are contradictory. *The Random House Dictionary* lists five usages under myth, two of which are descriptive of mythology as a story form relevant to the study of religion ("a traditional or legendary story, usually concerning some superhuman being . . . stories or matter of this kind") and three which indicate usage of myth as a term of evaluation ("invented . . . , imaginative or fictitious . . . , unproved collective belief that is accepted uncritically").[1]

On the one hand, we see that myth refers to a culture's traditional stories about the world and, on the other hand, to the rejection of the truth of those stories. Yet neither category of usage nor any of the five items listed/by *The Random House Dictionary* defines "myth" as it is being used in the title of this seminar, "Myth and the Crisis of Historical Consciousness." Our usage does not treat myth as something which cannot be believed in any way, as admitted fabrication. However, neither do most of the members of the group seem willing to restrict its application to stories, but refer rather to all non-literal or non-analytical conceptualization.

In this essay I shall argue that an understanding of the religious conceptions of mankind can best be served by restricting the use of "myth" to stories, thus dividing the larger area sometimes called "myth" in religious studies jargon into two sections, one of which has material in narrative form and the other in what might be called systematic form. Please do not let the words obscure the meaning. I could make a neologism to serve the same purpose, but I find that practice presumptuous and often unnecessary. Nevertheless, words do not heed commands and will continue to ramble all over *Random House*'s five and many other definitions despite what I say. For part of this essay, therefore, I shall resort to locutions such as "myth as narrative" in order to set the special definition in our minds.

As if the problems of definition were not enough, this essay will review the history of the phenomenon of myth in Western culture in order to understand why the word has meant the strangely opposite things to which the dictionaries refer and to see how the problem of myth has affected the history of religious thought. Finally I might be able to shed some light on the situation today from the perspective of the historical background and comment on how one can believe a myth.

MYTH AS NARRATIVE

It is possible to say that other things, i.e., doctrines, notions, pictures, etc., can function like myths did in their heyday without confusing the forms involved. However, it is clearly possible, and I think it is significant to note, that all the functions and every aspect of those functions might not be the same if the form is different. Myths and non-narrative worldviews may be alike in that they consist of "an indispensable symbol-set . . . which make an ultimately important although logically non-demonstrable truth claim."[2] But they are not alike in the ways in which they operate. A worldview is a more specific thing — it is more intellectual and less psychological than myth as narrative. It is also less ambiguous. "Worldview" implies a set of pictures of the world of which one can become self-conscious. On the other hand, myth is changed and some of it is lost when one attempts to translate it into discursive form or equate it with a specific set of meanings — a process which I will call "reduction" to emphasize the change and the loss involved.

While insisting that "myth" can be restricted to narrative form, I do not want to follow Eliade and others in restricting it to certain content, i.e., creation stories, or the pattern of the eternal return.[3] Likewise the story does not have to be about the gods to be a myth. Thus, a narrative myth can concern events thought to be historical in the past or the future, and can be man-centered as well as god(s)-centered. The biography of Jesus qualifies as narrative myth (or even myths, since it contains many smaller coherent units); also accounts of the end of the world, the *Iliad*, histories of the American revolution, and much more are seen to be mythic in form while not in the content specified by some usages of "myth." Myth, furthermore, does not require any one philosophical orientation or one type of worldview. It is not inevitably linked, for example, to a three-story universe or any other scheme doomed to rejection in light of scientific observation.

We cannot stop with form when defining myth, however. Of those things that have narrative form only those are myths which function in a special way, comparable to the function of any believed philosophy or worldview. Obviously it is possible for something which is a myth in form not to function mythically, just as, on the other hand, ideas or non-narrative world pictures can be said to function like effective myths. Something may have the form of myth but function as entertainment or become merely part of the traditional baggage of a culture. However, it is also possible, and here it becomes interestingly complicated, for a narrative myth to have a kind of half-function by being reduced to another form.

Thus there are three possibilities for dealing with the myths of one's culture: (1) One can reject a myth's sometime function as a provider of knowledge about the world (keeping the stories if at all for antiquarian, archaeological, or purely aesthetic purposes). (2) One can reduce a myth to more specific, non-narrative, meanings and hold them to have truth value, thus believing the myth in a derived form. (3) It is yet a third thing to believe (find the truth in) myth (narrative) as myth (recognizing its special form and function), without reduction or diminution.

It is not helpful to include all stories in the category of myth, even those stories which once were myths functionally, since the interesting thing about myths is their role as a provider of a sense of truth about the way things are. Therefore myth as narrative (the formal definition) is joined with myth as a vehicle of ultimate meaning (the functional definition) to produce the concept I find most helpful. Myths are stories which are believed to be more than mere stories; they are held to be ultimately true. (Note that myths cannot be created as such but only perceived or received as myths — a story becomes a myth in the special way it functions for those who rehearse it.)

BELIEVER'S INTERPRETATIONS OF MYTH

Three possible ways of dealing with myth were listed above, but in reverse chronological order. Believing myth as myth seems to be the oldest stage, followed by believing myth in some reduced, derived form, after which myths are fairy tales and entertainment if anything. We will return to a consideration of the first stage much later; the third would involve us in a discussion of the possible mythic functions of art. Our main problem now is distinguishing belief in reduced form from believing myth as myth.

It is by no means a recent phenomenon for people to reject the truth-value of myths or to take them in what has been called "broken" form. Classical Greek culture and Hellenistic cosmopolitanism both took myths to be something less than immediately true and yet somehow not completely false. They were as much aware as we are in the modern Western world of the multiplicity of myths in various cultures, and were as much embarrassed and confused that their ancestors apparently found ultimate meaning in such strange stories. The ancient thinkers variously reduced myths to historical (Euhemerism), physical (astrology), or moral notions, under the assumption that analytical thought had uncovered rather than demeaned or changed the true essence of myth.[4]

The brokenness of myth consists in its appropriation via a new or different form. It is not merely a matter of a broken or split consciousness, one part of which believes while the other part is aware of the specificity, undemonstrability, or just plain confusion of that belief. Nor do I think that brokenness is best understood by reference to "differentiation,"[5] which I take to be a sorting out of previously mixed veiled notions. Brokenness has been compared with naïveté or even Lévy-Bruhl's "participation mystique" in a way which assumes a radical difference between so-called primitive (myth-believing) thought and the sophisticated, complex thought of the Greek philosophers and their heirs. I even doubt the assumption of such primal naïveté, but that is not the problem of this essay.

The primary device used by the Hellenistic thinkers to derive acceptable ideas from myths was allegory. In Jewish and Christian thought the first prominent name is Philo, and New Testament exegesis of the Old uses this method also. Allegory permits one to dismiss the myth as story and substitute for it a set of ideas. Whether the story is true or not becomes irrelevant, especially insofar as the question of the historicity of biblical accounts is concerned. The truth lies at another level, in the lessons which can be preached on the basis of the story.

Distinctions can be made between rank allegory that has little or no connections with the original story and more sensitive interpretations. When the interpretation replaces the myth, however, we are faced with a situation comparable to the replacement of a poem by its prose summary or a painting by a photograph. Is there not something unique about the original and its special form which prevents it from simply being dismissed?

The reduction of myth to doctrine is, like allegory, in effect a new creation and a substitution. The *Upanishads* represent the same reduction, now in India, of myth and its ritual counterpart to ideas about man and the world. These ideas then become salutary and the former vehicles of religious interest are at first used, then tolerated, and finally forgotten. The relationship of the new element, doctrine, is often tangential to anything in the original myth. In fact it must be so in many such periods of transformation since the old myth no longer speaks the truth to many people. They do not, it must be emphasized, substitute myth with another myth in narrative form, but with another mode of religious perception and expression. This new mode may function like myth insofar as it is held with conviction and faith, but it no longer has the form of myth and cannot, therefore, function in all ways like it.

Allegorization and the reduction of myth to doctrine are ancient forms of demythologization and they remain popular into the twentieth century. Bultmann's only significant departure from his predecessors in basic method consists in being honest about the rejection of myth, as narrative form, and this honesty has given rise to most of the criticism. It is not quite fair to say that he has remythologized the Bible, in that he has not put it again into story form. Those who use "myth" to refer to any worldview have stumbled over this supposed inconsistency in Bultmann.[6] There are other problems in his thought but this is not one of them: he has not remythologized, although he has substituted a new set of meanings for the popular allegorizations and reductions of the past.

Because the allegory and the doctrinal interpretations both replace myth with discursive ideas, they are both difficult to criticize on the basis of the myth alone. How can one judge whether the new "level" of meaning is correct or not? It seems to me that there is no way of definitively reducing myth to doctrine. If one substitutes the doctrine for the myth as the Roman church has been accused of doing, one is locked into particular, time-bound philosophies or thought-worlds and the continued life and growth of the tradition is endangered. If the myth alone is considered to be revelatory, however, allegory and interpretation can replace each other with relative freedom. The only necessity in this case is maintaining some kind of convincing connection between the myth and the theology or preaching which are thought to emerge from it.

What usually happens in the replacement of interpretation by interpretation in the history of myth's influence is not necessarily a compounding of blatant misuse or error, with or without corrective reforms. It is more often a matter of partial vision following partial vision — aspects or valences of the myth perceived piecemeal and seriatim. It is a relatively rare age that has so little connection with the basic power of its mythology and yet so much reverence for it that it will insist that the myth means something absolutely incompatible with the earlier effects of the myth.

In the nineteenth century the desire to find meaning in Christian myths was especially poignant. The doctrines previously derived from this mythology seemed increasingly irrelevant to the emerging industrial world, and yet many people retained a sense of respect for the traditional stories, for the Bible, and for the image of Jesus. The power of the story of Jesus and therefore its mythic function were found in its role as an example for the moral life, much as the ancient Greeks interpreted their waning mythology in moralistic terms.[7] True, this approach was a tool of the dominant concern for morality in nineteenth century liberal theology, but the notion of a biographical paradigm was introduced and this signals a somewhat new way of reading myth. The new imitation of Christ was not a detailed but a general thing to be derived somehow from the course of Jesus' life in the Gospels.

This new perception of myth really thinks of it in terms of powerful fiction. Just as novels or plays can present patterns of human experience which are of greater significance than the particular people and setting of the portrayed events, so the life of Jesus or other stories could have the ring of eternal truth about them in the midst of ancient and irrelevant detail. When pressed, however, the believer in myth as fiction often resorts to translating the story into lessons or doctrines, a process which makes literature didactic. The good novel or the myth is more than an illustration for an otherwise conceivable truth — this much many people have sensed. The search continues through the twentieth century, therefore, to find a way of affirming the truth of myth.

The Scholarly Study of Myth

The history of the interpretation or reduction of its mythology by Western civilization is for the most part a search for personally acceptable truth. In the eighteenth century, however, ways of understanding myth began to emerge which worked on quite different principles. By this time ancient, non-Christian mythology had progressed to the third stage, that of cultural baggage and marginal entertainment value, while Jewish and Christian mythology was still being diligently reinterpreted and reduced to what theologians hoped would be acceptable theological ideas. Meanwhile a new attitude and approach to myth was being developed by scholars who wanted to understand the mythology of other peoples (and eventually also the mythology of their own culture), but now academically and objectively. They were not interested (primarily, at least) in believing myths, but in understanding how and why others apparently did. They reduced myth in a different way from that of the believer to components or notions which they could imagine someone else believing.

Since that time a number of scholarly approaches to myth have been espoused. I will not review all of the kinds of interpretation which have been offered to explain either the entire phenomenon of religion or mythology. Many would seem to dismiss entirely the possibility of believing myths personally once their true purpose was known, such as the promotion of social cohesion, the perpetuation of caste privilege, the intimidation of the young, etc., although these theories offer ample reason for men to try to get others to believe myths. Other scholarly approaches, on the other hand, do indicate ways in which myth might be believed in reduced form.

One approach assumes that mythology operated in primitive societies as its worn-out stage of fairy tale operates for contemporary children. Myths are an aspect of the childhood of mankind. This theory explains the unusual evocative powers of myth, and the strange sense of truth that they often elicit, as aspects of the role of childhood in personal development. People who believe myths are relatively more childlike than those who discard myths for straight, clear perceptions of reality. The world itself is increasingly coming of age as more and more people abandon, albeit reluctantly and nostalgically, the intellectual stuff of half-grown psyches — so says this kind of theory. However, it is less obvious today that Western civilization has matured; nostalgia is "in" and, therefore, this approach is not as popular as it once was.

Another way to understand how people might believe myths is represented by Jung and his followers. The archetypes of the human psyche which Jung saw in myths and in the minds of his patients were not doctrines or lessons. They did not say how the world should or could be, present a soteriological goal or way, or inspire moral activity. They were basic images of how life felt and how it aided or resisted one's movement. Take, for example, Neumann's study of the goddess where woman, earth, intellect, death, and life are discovered in the various myths concerning prominent goddesses.[8] The resulting picture in Neumann's book is too neat and systematic to be an adequate reflection on the jagged, ambiguous forms of the myths themselves, but the principles of this way of reading myth are clear. Myths have meaning like dreams, and vice-versa. They are stories because one sees one's life as a story, or better, a series of and overlapping of stories. Not just the biography of the nineteenth century with its focus on social and conscious events but the inner life of a man too are the subject of stories with mythic power.

One of the best expositions of this approach to myth is Campbell's study of the hero.[9] Some would say that his subject is more epic than myth, but not according to the definition being used here. The emphasis in Campbell's analysis of hero myths is placed on the progress of the story, not just on the basic images or characters, an advance over many Jungian studies which break myths into static moments. A story is more than a series of relationships; there is a constant movement toward or away from things, through situations and around them, which constant attention to images and symbols ignores.

Seeing myths as expressions of the psychic life of man has permitted a great number of modern men to admit their fascination with myth. The popularity of books with this approach — even of the coffee table variety — attests to the power of this appropriation of myth. As story, its basic form, the myth remains important. Its significance is not so much intellectualized as emotionalized. There are problems with this reading of myth, nevertheless.

It seems to me that the Jungian approach tends too much to imitate the traditional religious and intellectual appropriations of myth which, as an objective study, it should explain. It tends to universalize the images and symbols of myth and dream, assuming that all men, or at least all men in a certain cultural tradition, will have basically the same psychic materials. The archetypes become metaphysical in stature and require an act of faith, to be recognized as such. In this the pluralism of the ancient and modern worlds, which created the dilemma of belief in myth to begin with, is collapsed by a new affirmation of unity. A way of believing myth is produced which does not differ very much from the traditional religious affirmation that myth (in general now, rather than particular myths) is revelatory of a body of absolute truth.

The Jungians imitate the intellectualization of myth by their abstracting from myths only those aspects which support an independently derived theory of man. Their view of man is better than many for purposes of commenting on myth, but it remains a separable and ideational matter after all. It is not myth as myth that the Jungian practitioner, patient, or student believes, but Jungian philosophy as illustrated by myths.

A third type of myth interpretation proceeds from the notion that myth has meaning comparable to if not identical with the meaning of art. The arts can function like myths, giving a sense of ultimate truths. And since literature is often in narrative form, it can be identical in form and function with the myths of primitive peoples and the religious traditions. Thus the theater becomes a church, and various novels become bibles for certain individuals. The possibilities for aesthetic analysis in these instances recapitulates the list of believers' and scholars' ways of finding meaning in myth, i.e., reduction to ideas, allegorization, psychologization, etc. However, as the philosophy of art turns from literature and the graphic arts as the typical locus of aesthetic questions to music and more abstract forms of literature and painting, it raises new possibilities for the understanding of myth beyond those summarized above.

Susanne Langer attempts to understand music as the basis for her aesthetics and consequently develops a theory of art in which the form itself is meaning.[10] The vocabulary of music with its meanings due to association and convention is comparable to the symbolism of myth; and the essentially musical meaning is a matter of the relationship of these parts to each other and to the whole, at any point and in motion. Myth in such a perspective means its structure, and reveals the possible relationship of things.

Students of religion know this kind of analysis more from reading Lévi-Strauss than Langer. In many essays the French anthropologist has analyzed myths in terms of their structure, indicating also that the meaning of myth lies in the relationship of its parts.[11] Both Langer and Lévi-Strauss arouse reactions of incredulity at first. One wonders how something as dynamic and attractive as myth could really be so simple and abstract as structure. The point is that structure is more important than we think, and that other apsects of myth may be less essential to its power than its structure.

The structural analysis of myth is based on the notion that men replicate their basic patterns of relationship and action in many levels or areas of endeavor. A myth or a piece of music may elicit a sense of meaning or significance because it exhibits a structure that has echoes or further exemplification in ritual activity, social behavior, political consciousness, and any number of other manifestations of human consciousness. The symbols of the myth or the work of art may have fascinating assocations by themselves, especially because of their use in yet other structural expressions in which they resonate. Hence the symbol abstracted from many contexts seems to have a life of its own in its capability for revalorization. In the myth or other contextual form, however, the symbol acts primarily as a function in the whole and should not be isolated in our investigation.

The clearest examples of this approach for me are Lévi-Strauss' analysis of totemism[12] and Mary Douglas' understanding of the ancient Hebrew food and body regulations.[13] Totemism was understood for years in terms of the various animals, plants, and other objects which functioned as totems. Lévi-Strauss, however, shows that these items were much more a matter of familiar nomenclature for expressing the organization of society and the variously conceived divisions of the world. Douglas likewise sorts through a number of theories about what separates clean from unclean in the Torah and concludes that they generally miss the point. She proposes instead that the Hebrews had a concern for wholeness and the preservation of boundaries which was manifest in the structure of and mutually reinforced by ritual regulations and political consciousness.

Myths can have meaning of a profound nature while perceived as structure or pattern because they reach every area of human consciousness, not just society or art, or what is narrowly defined to be religion. If anything in human life has meaning myth does, as the dominant exemplification of the structures of consciousness. Far from being a devious or reducible form of what exists more really on another level, myth is often the force in human consciousness that makes the other aspects fall into line. Far from mirroring other aspects of life, myth is the single most influential force in the determination of the patterns of the rest of life.

The structuralist understanding and appreciation of myth is based on its total form as narrative. It does not so much replace interpretations based on the isolated symbols of myth as add to them and put them in second place. It should not surprise us that myth has many ways of being significant, for it is often the cumulative effect of hints at meaning that give the sense of truth.

A Note on Believing Myth through Drugs

A new category is demanded, I think, by the recent phenomenon of validating mythology by the experiences of the mind under the influence of psychedelic drugs. Some have become believers in myth; others have argued that drugs (e.g., soma) or states of mind like drug-induced states were involved in the origination of ancient myths.[14] In either case we are confronted with an empirical validation of myth and thus a way of believing myths which goes beyond dreams into the mysteries of the human psyche.

This way of believing myth differs from all those above precisely because it is experiential. The mystic always could say, of course, that he saw and heard the myth or its characters directly. Now a special variation of that claim is being made. (The contemporary drug subculture has a bit of its own mythology, in Kerouac's novels and the like, but that is not the issue here.) The way to believe myth via this approach is to experience once more through the agency of drugs the mental distortion and/or expansion which led to mythopoeia originally.

There does not seem to be any way of denying the validity of the experience of truth based on personal experience, although I agree with William James that it remains a matter of individual, private validation.[15] A sense of conviction in those who do not have the experience can come only from a recognition of authority and a faith in the one who has the special experience.

Myth and the Crisis of Historical Consciousness

My definition of myth and survey of the varieties of interpretation, reduction, and analysis, leads me to three conclusions regarding the theme of our seminar. First, inability to believe in myth as myth is not a new phenomenon, being at least as old as the *Upanishads*. Since the reinterpretation, translation, and reduction of myths begins so long ago, and in cultures which are not concerned with history (India and Greece), I conclude that the problem of finding meaning in myth and the development of historical awareness should not be related in a one-to-one fashion. There are many reasons why myths should lose significance or change in their modes of influence or apprehension, only one of which is the shifting of attention to history. Likewise, today, in the partial collapse of historical consciousness, myth is not the only alternative.

My use of the term "myth" and analysis of its role is based on and corroborates the assumption that religion is not one thing but many. There are at least what can be called different styles of religion or different ways of being religious. The mythic style is only one of them. The others include the intellectual style which reduces myths to ideas, as well as the ritual-ethical style which concentrates on behavior. To these could be added the devotional style, the communal, and many subdivisions or new categories which it is not the purpose of this essay to define. What characterizes the mythic style is fascination in detail with the myth, periodic rehearsal and ritual expression of the myth, the portrayal of the world in terms of myths, and its very unwillingness to reduce the myths to anything else. Of course this style is ancient and does not dominate any religious tradition today. That does not make it an impossibility in the modern world, however — only a rarity in its pure form and a minor element in many mixes of piety. Thus we should not dichotomize the believing world into mythic and historical consciousness, but recognize the many styles of religion, some of which are confused with each other because of their common use of myths and the too-broad use of the term "myth" by scholars.

The second conclusion to which this study has brought me, and which is based much more closely on the analysis in the above paragraphs, concerns the variety of ways in which people subscribe to truth in myths. Most people seem to believe in doctrinal systems (or loose federations of ideas about the world and God) rather than the myths upon which they are supposedly based. This explains the relative biblical ignorance of otherwise pious Christians — they do not so much believe this repository of myths as the interpretations that they or others have made from it. When terms like "mythic consciousness" are used to denote what is really a reduction of a mythology to ideas (whether one's own mythology or another's is involved), the myths have been side-stepped already. The tendency to avoid the myth as story is corrected by the structural approach, however, and this corrective is one of the most valuable aspects of structural studies today.

Third, and finally: What can be concluded about believing myth as myth today? Has pluralism like that which made the Greeks first aware of the peculiarity of their mythology, or shifts in values like those which led in India to the new religious style of the *Upanishads*, or historical consciousness which has warred against some of the mythological elements in the Jewish and Christian traditions, made believing myth as myth impossible? This essay does not demonstrate but perhaps illustrates that contemporary man can come to a new respect for myth precisely because of his historical insight. If in the course of history myths have meant so much in so many ways, and if they continue to yield insights into man's understanding of himself as a meaning-producing animal, one indeed can believe in myth as myth, but now as a source of new interpretations. Mythology in general can be expected to yield ever more and different kinds of information about man's experience of the world, and specific myths will function as guides for men concerning the meaning of life and the best way to live.

To believe in something is to be convinced of its authority and efficacy. To see myth as a continuing source of insight is to give it authority. To be willing to respond to a myth in action and attitude is to take it with conviction. Such responses depend on the assumption that myth is always more than any reduction, interpretation, or analysis — that it stands beyond what we make of it in any way or even in all the ways put together.

Believing myth as myth does not mean a return to a primal naïveté, which I doubt ever existed anyway and is part of modern man's misguided apprehension of the "primitive" world. Nor does it mean believing myth in yet another derived form, e.g., a new set of doctrines more or less based on myths. I do not even think that we have to change our mode of consciousness in order to find meaning in myths as well as history and science. We need only broaden the world of our data, have a fuller notion of what makes up reality, and include the uniquely human and psychic elements of life in our notion of the factual. Then the old polarities of myth and fact, religion and science, revelation and rationality disappear. Myth is seen to be as ordinary and as extraordinary as any other attempt to express the mystery of the world, and as fruitful.

NOTES

[1]*The Random House Dictionary* (1966).

[2]W. Taylor Stevenson, "Myth and the Crisis of Historical Consciousness," collected in this volume. The exact quotation is taken from the first draft of the seminar paper.

[3]Mircea Eliade, *Cosmos and History: The Myth of the Eternal Return* (New York: Harper and Row, 1959), pp. 43ff.

[4]Jean Seznec, *The Survival of the Pagan Gods* (Princeton: Princeton University Press, 1953), pp. 3-147.

[5]Stevenson, "Myth and the Crisis," p. 4, *et passim*.

[6]W. Taylor Stevenson, *History as Myth* (New York: Seabury Press, 1969), p. 92. Note that it is again a matter of definition: Stevenson's definition of myth and mine arise from different concerns, and thus the results are different.

[7]Gustaf Aulen, *Christus Victor* (New York: Macmillan Publishing Co., Inc., 1969), p. 134.

[8]Erich Neumann, *The Great Mother* (New York: Pantheon Books, 1963).

[9]Joseph Campbell, *The Hero with a Thousand Faces* (New York: World Books, 1956).

[10]Susanne Langer, *Philosophy in a New Key* (New York: Charles Scribner's Sons, 1953), p. 27.

[11]Claude Lévi-Strauss, *Structural Anthropology* (Garden City, New York: Doubleday and Co., 1967), pts. 3 and 4.

[12]Claude Lévi-Strauss, *Totemism* (Boston: Beacon Press, 1963).

[13]Mary Douglas, *Purity and Danger* (Baltimore: Penguin Books, 1970), chaps. 3 and 7.

[14]Mary Barnard, *The Mythmakers* (Athens, Ohio: Ohio University Press, 1966).

[15]William James, *The Varieties of Religious Experience* (New York: New American Library, 1961), pp. 332ff.

DEMCO